Vocabulary Connections

Vocabulary Connections

A Structured Approach to Deepening Students' Academic and Expressive Language

Mary Ehrenworth

Routledge
Taylor & Francis Group

NEW YORK AND LONDON

A Stenhouse Book

Cover images by Getty
Cover llustrations by Jennifer Zanghi

First published 2025
by Routledge
605 Third Avenue, New York, NY 10158

and by Routledge
4 Park Square, Milton Park, Abingdon, Oxon, OX14 4RN

Routledge is an imprint of the Taylor & Francis Group, an informa business

© 2025 Mary Ehrenworth

Credits for borrowed material begin on page 211.

ISBN: 978-1-032-82695-0 (pbk)
ISBN: 978-1-003-51375-9 (ebk)

DOI: 10.4324/9781003513759

Typeset in Chaparral Pro
by KnowledgeWorks Global Ltd.

*For Dina Ercolano, Janice Liao, Betsy Piombo, and Katie Diamond,
and the entire educational force of luminaries at P.S. 158, NYC, including
Jennifer Zanghi, whose illustrations across this text add to the beauty of this work*

Contents

Acknowledgments

Thank you to the teachers, literacy coaches, and school leaders who love words and have played with, invented, and revised so many of these lessons. Thank you to the learners of all ages who have contributed their insights and their work. It is such a delight to frolic with language among like-minded friends.

Thank you to my editor, Terry Thompson, whose patience and perspicuity guided every aspect of this project. Terry is a beautiful teacher as well as a writer and editor. That knowledge of children and classrooms permeates Terry's editing, as does his commitment to equity and inclusion and representation. All of this work is more elegant, as is the world, for being permeated with Terry Thompson.

And thank you to the entire team at Stenhouse and Routledge, including Melanie Moy, who kept us organized and supported all the visual representations, and who was crucial to this project. I'd also like to thank Claire Bell for her extraordinary powers of copy-editing, and Elizabeth Spicer for taking the proofs through production.

I want to thank colleagues at a few schools. P.S. 158, in Manhattan, led by the dauntless Principal Dina Ercolano, Assistant Principal Janice Liao, and Instructional Coaches Betsy Piombo and Katie Diamond—thank you, leaders, for always wanting to explore new ideas, and thank you teachers, for diving into vocabulary explorations, for giving feedback, for sharing the quirky and fabulous work your students author. Thank you as well to the brilliant Lara Stein for leading us all into morphology work and teaching us how magical it could be! Thank you as well to P.S. 267, also in Manhattan, led by Principal Medea McEvoy and Assistant Principal Farah Chowdry, who give teachers so much permission to innovate. Thank you to teachers there, who especially helped to hone these lessons on literary vocabulary. And thank you to George M. Davis Elementary School, in New Rochelle. Principal Anthony Brambola and Literacy Coach Kelly Neault, you sponsored study groups on vocabulary, and teachers, you and your students showed us the joy children take in learning words and how they work! Thank you for sharing your students' lovely work as well.

A few educators whom I must name. Audra Robb, Literacy and Humanities Curriculum Specialist at United Nations International School—Audra's footprints are in this work, in the delectation with language, and specifically in Audra's "characters collide" idea, which has been such an engaging way to think about how characters influence each other. And Marc Todd, co-author and teacher at I.S. 289 in Manhattan. Marc's work on criticality, especially in investigating word choice in social studies and the linguistic and colonial heritage of names, is foundational to thinking about vocabulary and power, and seeking decolonizing spaces in our classrooms and through our pedagogy.

Thank you to Marta Magellan and Mauro Magellan for the incredible nonfiction science books they create for children, along with photographer James Gersing. Thank you as well to publisher Penny Eifrig of Eifrig Publishing, for bringing books into the world that get children to fall in love with nature and science.

And I want to thank organizations. First, thank you to all at *De Mots et de Crais*, especially founder Yves Nadon and my co-conspirator, Diane Oullette, but also to every member, for the ravishing pleasure of thinking and learning with you, and for all you have taught me about the French language and multilingualism. Thank you to colleagues at the American School of Barcelona, especially Director Mark Pingitore, Director of Teaching and Learning Johanna Cena, Literacy Coach and Consultant Jenny Killion, and every marvelous teacher, for your curiosity, your playfulness, and your dedication.

And thank you to all the colleagues I've treasured at Teachers College, whose wisdom informs this work, and whose collaboration and love make all things possible. Thank you to Emily Butler Smith for leading with such grace. Thank you to Katy Wischow and Kristin Smith for reveling in vocabulary and revealing its delights! Thank you to Mary Ann Mustac for supporting all my work and endeavors. Thank you to Lisa Cazzola for arranging learning environments and collaborations. Thank you to Amanda Hartman for helping us strive for more culturally responsive pedagogies. Thank you to Alexandra Roman for insisting that multilingualism be front and center and for exploring vocabulary instruction in multilingual settings with me. Thank you to Lauren Gould for sharing not only incredible gifts for design, but all of her creative thinking. Thank you to Heather Burns for fostering every new idea and making each better. Thank you to Kate Roberts and Chris Lehman and Katherine Bomer for inspiring me to outgrow myself. And thank you to each and every member of this learning community, whether you are in the halls of Teachers College or dispersed to illuminate educational frontiers around the planet. It is a privilege to learn with you.

Finally, thank you to Jenny Zanghi, teacher extraordinaire at P.S. 158, and the remarkable illustrator for this project. Jenny, your drawings of Monarch butterflies and Etymological maps are stunning. Every visual you created adds to the power and beauty of Vocabulary Connections. But your collaboration has been about more than the prodigious powers you bring with colored pencils and markers. You bring a sense of possibility and wonder that is contagious and beautiful and I am so very, very lucky to write and work with you.

Introduction
A Structured Approach to Deepening Students' Academic and Expressive Vocabulary

One of the most beautiful things about reading, in any language, is that you gather literary and domain language as you read. Researchers call this process *incidental learning*. Of course this isn't the only reason to read. Reading takes you to places of deep familiarity and unsettling dissonance. Reading comforts and disturbs. Reading can offer a haven or send you off on uncharted escapades. Reading makes you dauntless and wise and humble. And, in addition to this, reading expands your vocabulary. This is one of the greatest gifts you can give your students—the opportunity to read deeply and widely. Your students will learn more, and they will have more literary and domain language to express what they know as they learn from sources who have more knowledge than they do—essentially, they learn new vocabulary through the languages of books.

Every book we share with our learners will teach them something, and every book will teach them new words. Linguist Elfrieda Hiebert describes this process in one of my favorite texts, *Teaching Words and How They Work*, saying: "it is in texts that human beings have traditionally stored their knowledge." She adds: "texts can be a source of equity and opportunity" (Hiebert, 2020, 2). In another essential text, *Shifting the Balance: 6 Ways to Bring the Science of Reading into the Upper Elementary Classroom*, Cunningham, Burkins, and Yates solidify this assertion, stating: "the lexical richness students encounter through texts is a vital source of new vocabulary" (Cunningham, Burkins, and Yates, 2023, 80). As children read, they acquire more sophisticated vocabulary, and as they acquire vocabulary, complex texts become more comprehensible. Deep reading and vocabulary acquisition are a gorgeous, reciprocal relationship.

When I was a new teacher, I thought that reading itself would be enough in terms of supporting students' vocabulary acquisition. I had this idea that all my students would harvest a glorious array of words as they read Jacqueline Woodson and Christopher Paul Curtiss and J.K. Rowling. And many students did reap linguistic benefits from their reading—they read so much, and so attentively, that their incidental learning was like rocket fuel for vocabulary growth. But I was less aware, then, of readers who were currently reading below benchmark, whose books offered them more limited word choice. I had fewer multilingual learners then and I knew less about developing all of their linguistic competencies. All of which is to say, I wish I had done more to develop my students' vocabulary alongside and outside of their reading.

But what I've come to learn is that, with a few intentional shifts, we can teach vocabulary by incorporating a handful of methods and taking advantage of structures and curriculum that are already in play in our classrooms—all while grounding our conversations in the reading, writing, and content area work we do every day. We will probably have to dedicate a little bit of time specifically to etymology and morphology, but most literary and academic vocabulary can be taught through engaging read-alouds, shared reading, book clubs, and content studies. And you will be so **pleased/content/ delighted/gratified/chuffed** at the results!

The truth is that increasing children's vocabulary has a profound, positive impact on all aspects of their learning. Students who collect domain (expert, content) vocabulary increase their content knowledge. Students who know how to figure out words from subtle context clues can read and learn from harder nonfiction. Students who control literary language can express more nuanced ideas about stories. Students who understand morphology can figure out hundreds of new words from familiar prefixes, suffixes, and roots. Students who grasp cognates recognize and can infer meaning across languages. Students who pay attention to word choice are more critical readers. Vocabulary acquisition intertwines with other learning in radical, symbiotic cognitive processes, especially when you focus on *usage* and *context*, so that children come to deep conceptual understandings of new terms, and they learn *how* to acquire vocabulary.

Connecting Vocabulary Research to Classroom Practice

There is an enormous amount of research on the significance of vocabulary acquisition, including the learning gains that accompany vocabulary growth, the kinds of vocabulary to focus our instruction on, how learners acquire vocabulary, as well as ways of thinking that will help us strive for humanizing, culturally responsive pedagogies. I love mulling over research and thinking about how to innovate pedagogy and classroom structures from theory. If you also love that, you may want to dive into some of the texts, articles, and studies that range from theories of language acquisition and multilingual learning to brain research on word learning, to linguistic analyses of text vocabulary to large studies of comprehension. You can visit this book's website (www.vocabularyconnections.org) to download a summary for closer study and links that will take you to some of the most recent and compelling research.

For now, there are a few ideas from research that feel tremendously important to consider, especially because some of these ideas interrupt old teaching practices. The first supports all we've covered so far: that reading comprehension and vocabulary growth are intertwined. Through everyday interactions, students encounter and use mostly what Beck et al. (2013) call Tier 1 words, or everyday, social language. When they read, students will encounter many Tier 2, or precise words, as well as Tier 3, or rare, specialized words. "The relationship between vocabulary and texts is reciprocal," Hiebert remarks. "Familiarity with the vocabulary of a text supports comprehension, while simultaneously texts are a primary source for gaining new vocabulary" (Hiebert, 2020, 2). When you make time for vocabulary instruction, know that you are also deepening reading comprehension.

A second idea is that a lot of literary vocabulary isn't in the stories children read (or not the high-leverage vocabulary that is worth creating instruction around). Instead, a lot of high-leverage literary vocabulary will come from words readers use to *talk about* stories. As they encounter multiple experiences with figurative language, idioms, and a rich palette of words in complex narratives (Hiebert, 2020, 80), your readers will acquire or approximate many of these words through incidental learning. But the really high-leverage instruction will be teaching students words to talk about the stories they read—to describe characters' traits and emotions, to talk about the setting, to analyze the mood. Hiebert calls these categories *semantic clusters* (Hiebert, 2020, 31). Most of these words aren't in the text—the reader needs to infer from the text and needs nuanced language to express their ideas. That's why direct instruction in literary vocabulary is so useful. Hiebert emphasizes how much more likely learners are to remember literary vocabulary, when they attach it to characters and stories they love.

Another important idea from research is that teaching children about the interior parts of words serves as a springboard to help them learn many words while, at the same time, aiding reading comprehension. In "The Science of Reading Comprehension Instruction," Nell Duke, Allessandra Ward, and P. David Pearson recommend teaching word-solving skills such as morphology to children, so that they can use these strategies as they read to increase comprehension (Duke, Ward, and Pearson, 2021). Cunningham, Burkins, and Yates (2023) also emphasize the importance of teaching word parts, offering teachers a useful tool for planning which prefixes, suffixes, and roots to teach in each grade—their "Multi-Year Plan for Systemic Morphology Instruction," which they generously share in the download section of their website (TheSixShifts.com).

A fourth significant idea is that domain vocabulary instruction should emerge from meaningful, engaging content studies. As with literary vocabulary, this research disrupts old habits of pre-teaching a few words that will come up in a nonfiction text children are about to read. Instead, these important findings encourage us to teach students how to collect domain vocabulary as part of building knowledge, and to teach them how to attend to the wide variety of context clues authors embed to alert readers to new concepts and terms. Tim Shanahan's post, "How I Teach Students to Use Context Clues in Vocabulary Learning," is one of the most persuasive arguments for providing students with passive scaffolding (transferable strategies for learning from context clues), rather than definitions, so that young readers become adept at attending to "word meaning in a comprehension-centric fashion." It's also extraordinary how many Tier 2 (precise) and Tier 3 (rare, specialized) words children will learn in content studies when they are invited to read and engage with topics deeply.

Finally, and most crucially, consider the idea that all of our pedagogies—including vocabulary instruction—should be inclusive, humanizing, affirming, and empowering. Sonia Cabell (2022) explains how making sure all students can access complex texts is itself an equity project. She states: "Complex text offers opportunities to develop academic language and acquire knowledge about the world." Cabell gives advice on choosing texts, on building text sets so students can move up levels, and on researching students' lives and funds of knowledge. In a similar vein, Sara Vogel and Ofelia García (2017) advocate for pedagogies that affirm and leverage students' diverse and dynamic language practices. They encourage educators to embrace translanguaging, where students reach for academic language in whatever language they can find the most sophisticated and nuanced words, as a linguistic process, so that it is not the end goal but part of a process that leads to growth in academic vocabulary across languages.

Supporting Instruction Through Vocabulary Connections

This book is designed to give you practical, usable structures and ideas to connect this important research in intentional ways. I've ordered the sections of the book, the chapters, and their lessons in a sequence that has been successful for me when embedding this work alongside meaningful reading instruction, but you can adjust the order as you consider the needs of your students and plan around your curriculum. The three overarching sections of the book include: literary vocabulary, word consciousness, and domain vocabulary.

Literary Vocabulary

Imagining that, often, you'll start your year with reading aloud captivating narratives, Chapter 1 begins with teaching students **literary vocabulary**. You'll set learners up to collect words to describe characters in the stories you read to them, so that all your students can immediately engage in this work, regardless of their reading proficiency. In fact, you'll begin with digital narratives—short, award-winning animated videos such as Pixar's *Joy and Heron*. You'll teach nuanced literary vocabulary, in context, so that your readers develop more expressive language for their ideas about characters. One beautiful effect of this instruction is that your readers will also develop more nuanced interpretations. Thinking about how Heron seems **defiant** and **cunning** at the beginning of the story, but **protective** and **generous** by the end, is about more than applying literary vocabulary. It involves thinking about character change, about perspective, and about hidden sides of characters.

All of the lessons in Chapter 1 offer opportunities to connect to read-alouds. As students deepen and extend their literary vocabulary and their interpretation skills over time, they can begin to apply strategies from those lessons through additional practice during independent reading and book club conversations.

Chapter 2 continues to focus on literary vocabulary, and shifts to writing about reading, specifically sketchnoting, as a way to explore more nuanced ideas about characters, to use precise words to express these ideas, and to develop close reading skills. This work is probably most useful in book clubs, where preparation deepens discussion, and where writing about reading becomes meaningful because it is part of collective interpretation. If your students won't be in book clubs, you can attach this work to independent reading, to shared reading, or to read-aloud. The lessons in Chapter 2 don't have to follow immediately after those of Chapter 1. For example, you could return to literary vocabulary and writing about reading as a way to explore close reading of narratives at any point in the year.

Word Consciousness

The section on **word consciousness** follows literary vocabulary. You can wait to begin teaching these lessons until you have launched literary vocabulary, or you can start these lessons simultaneously. The lessons in Chapter 3 and 4 are not attached directly to reading a specific text and you'll need to dedicate about ten minutes once or twice a week to this instruction. The sooner you begin, the sooner children will start applying their knowledge of language to figuring out word parts and word meanings! Chapter 3 presents lessons on etymology, compound words, and cognates. It begins with teaching learners about the complex history of English, instilling an awareness of English as a malleable, ever-growing language, influenced by many sources. All of the lessons focus on children as word-decipherers and word creators. The work with cognates not only supports your multilingual learners in learning many words, it also helps all learners become more aware of linguistic crossovers across languages and cultures. There are some resources for Chapter 3 that you may want to download from the website (www.vocabularyconnections.org), such as compound word lists and cognate lists, as well as illustrated word cards for multilingual learners.

Chapter 4 explores morphology. It begins with a lesson on morphemes, and then it presents a replicable protocol for teaching prefixes, suffixes, and roots. One important note about the morphology lessons in this chapter is that each one is meant to be taught several times, for a group of prefixes, a group of suffixes, and a group of roots. You'll find the protocol, and recommendations for morpheme lists, at the start of the chapter. You'll also see the same attention to children as word creators, and on the website (www.vocabularyconnections.org), you'll find morpheme cards children can use to create words.

Domain Vocabulary

Chapters 5 and 6 turn to **domain vocabulary**—the expert, specialized vocabulary involved in learning about a topic. Plan these lessons for when students will be in content or nonfiction studies. They can be included as part of large-scale science or social studies content investigations, small research projects, or any kind of research-based writing endeavor. The lessons themselves model using some texts on Monarch butterflies, but can easily be adjusted for use regardless of the topic students or your learning community are researching. So, of course, feel free to shift out the demonstration texts. The lessons in Chapter 5 teach students to collect domain vocabulary, to sketch and label as a means of note taking, to collect and explain conceptual vocabulary, and to practice conceptual sorts.

The lessons of Chapter 6 show students how to attend to the kind of subtle context clues that proliferate in complex texts. The lessons use *Up, Up and Away, Monarch Butterflies*, written by Marta Magellan, with illustrations by Mauro Magellan and photographs by James Gersing. It is a marvelous text, the kind of nonfiction that respects children as learners and teaches significant science and expert, domain vocabulary, while enthralling them with beautiful illustrations, complex charts and diagrams, and fabulous nature photography. Each lesson teaches children how authors use varied and sometimes subtle context clues to teach their readers new terms and conceptual vocabulary. These lessons all focus on transfer—on teaching students how to use content clues in any complex nonfiction text. You can substitute other topics/texts for these lessons, and on the website (www.vocabularyconnections.org) you'll find a list of diverse nonfiction that especially rewards vocabulary instruction, while getting kids to fall in love with science and history.

Methods, Pedagogy, Assessment, and Standards

All of these lessons are intended to be replicable with multiple texts, in a variety of learning experiences and across any curriculum. As you plan and teach the lessons in these chapters, you'll develop replicable protocols for:

- collecting literary and domain vocabulary (Chapters 1, 5)

- writing about reading as a way to deepen vocabulary and interpretation (Chapter 2)

- investigating word choice as a way of thinking about point of view (Chapters 2, 6)

- exploring context clues in complex nonfiction (Chapter 6)

- building word consciousness—morphology, compound words, cognates (Chapters 3, 4)

Each of the *Vocabulary Connections* lessons incorporates *inquiry* and *direct instruction*—and you'll see a bit of both in every interaction. That is, in a lesson that is mostly inquiry, you'll explicitly teach some new words or parts of words, and in a lesson that is mostly direct instruction, there will be moments of inquiry, where students think of other, related words. You'll also attend to *visual cues—charts and tools*. Whether you share how a vertical suggests shades of meaning for words for feelings, how a semantic map suggests relationships between words and concepts, or how a morphology chart captures word parts, these visual cues offer easily accessed scaffolds to support your learners.

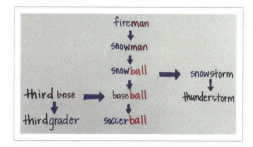

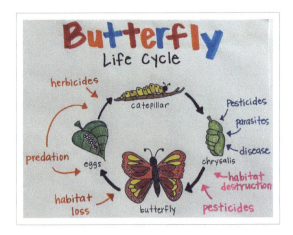

Each lesson also leads students toward achieving benchmarks on national and global standards. You'll find a section at the start of each chapter that connects its lessons to reading, speaking and listening, and language standards. As each state has made subtle adaptations to localize standards, I've included those adopted by most states, iterated from the CCSS (thecorestandards.org) and New York State's Next Generation Standards (nysed.gov/standards-instruction), which are almost identical to those of California and Massachusetts, and only differ in small ways from those of other states. You'll also see recommendations for assessment, focusing particularly on measuring application—how your young linguists apply the strategies you teach and the words they learn, in context and in fresh situations.

Classroom Structures to Support Vocabulary Connections

Throughout the lessons that follow, you'll notice several structures that are important for implementation. These structures support the work students will do in these lessons and, once established, further lessons you'll plan on your own beyond the work presented here. These include:

Talk partnerships

Talk partnerships foster student oral language practice centered on inquiry, understanding, and application. They also foster learning alliances—peer interdependent relationships, so that students learn from and with each other. In "Joyful Vocabulary Acquisition: Pedagogies for Developing Children's Literary Vocabulary (and Analysis of Characters in Narratives)" (2025), Lauren Gould, Alexandra Roman, and I describe how "learning alliances help children thrive by offering them smaller coalition groups inside of classroom spaces." These conversations allow learners to explore language in low-risk experiences, alongside peers they trust. In *Unearthing Joy: A Guide to Culturally and Historically Responsive Curriculum and Instruction*, Gholdy Muhammad (2023) explores humanizing pedagogies and educational spaces in which children thrive in joy. With these goals in mind, plan your linguistic partnerships in ways that wrap children in love and affirmation, and foster a sense of playfulness and coalition.

Thinking carefully about pairing learners in partnerships will help each student thrive. When you consider your multilingual learners, perhaps you'll pair them with students who share their languages, providing informal mentorship and coalition. Inside these multilingual partnerships, students may translanguage, sketch, label, and support each other's language acquisition. Sometimes, of course, students may benefit or prefer to work with a peer who speaks or writes their new language. In this case remember that you may not be fluent in Ukrainian, for example, nor is another student fluent in Ukrainian, but AI translation apps are. Lake and Beisly (2019) demonstrate how using translation apps can build relationships between teachers and students as well as among students, and can support multilingualism, engagement, and a sense of self-esteem. Find out which students enjoy learning new languages, or are adept with technology, as they can be learning allies in this type of partnership.

Book Clubs

Book clubs create a marvelous opportunity for students to apply all they've learned about collecting literary vocabulary and attending to nuanced interpretation with their more variety of expressive language.

Book clubs also provide reasons for students to write about their reading—another significant opportunity to explore and extend literary vocabulary usage. Teach readers strategies for sketchnoting and labeling with literary vocabulary (see Chapter 2), and they'll use these same techniques to prepare for book club conversations. Their discussions will be richer, because their vocabulary is more nuanced.

Research Clubs

Research clubs (or research partnerships) create opportunities for learners to investigate conceptual vocabulary together, to teach each other new domain words and new knowledge, to use their vocabulary learning and knowledge to read more complex texts, and to deepen their understanding together over time. Also, it's just more interesting to learn together. There is a reason that scientists work in teams. Each research partner brings their own perspective and fascinations. Together, students learn more than they would alone. And they have many more opportunities to talk and reasons to note-take.

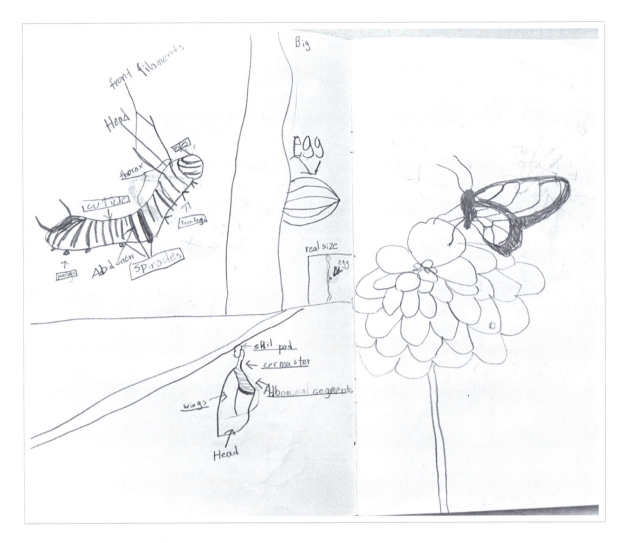

It's also magical to see how students who share their vocabulary collections and sketch-notes in research clubs have rich, text-based content discussions. The time spent learning to attend to important new vocabulary, to pay attention to context clues, to collect and explain the significance of new terms to each other, becomes part of how learners build knowledge—and how they teach others.

Vocabulary Walls, Charts, Tools, Digital Collections

Dedicate some space to display charts and tools that will help your learners recall the vocabulary they are learning—and the context as well—as these visual scaffolds will help with retention. Some possibilities include:

- **Charts** with word collections to describe specific characters in stories, so children can easily turn to these words as you revisit familiar characters and introduce new ones. You may reconsider your traditional word wall in favor of word collections that are grouped by meaning.

- **Verticals**—these are often useful in two forms. One form can be displayed as larger, visible word charts children can see during whole group conversations and read-alouds, with a second smaller, personal version that can be tucked into students' notebooks or books. Children often love to work with paint samples with color gradients that make for lovely verticals. They can also hand color their own with colored pencil. When you and your learners have verticals on hand, everyone reaches for more nuanced vocabulary.

- **Content collections**—during content studies, create a part of your vocabulary wall dedicated to that content. Include vocabulary collections, semantic maps, sketches and labels as models for note-taking. These visual records act as a kind of research bulletin board for all your learners, as well as providing extra support for multilingual learners. In time, you'll find that this dedicated wall space for collecting and displaying content vocabulary will become something you and your learners turn to frequently during read-alouds and class conversations.

| inconsolable |
| desolate |
| miserable |
| sad |
| downhearted |
| dejected |

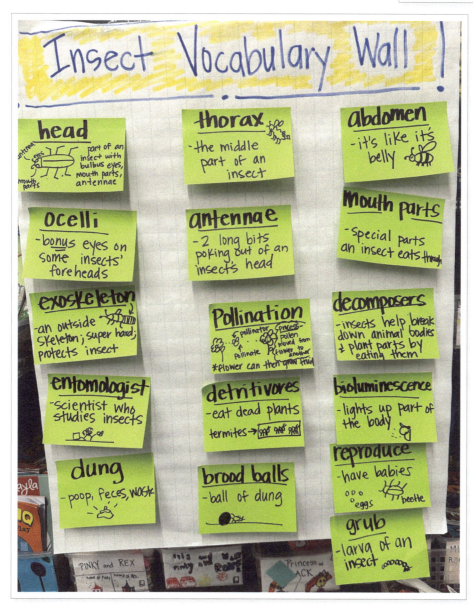

- **Digital tools** such as Lucid or FigJam allow you to create digital sticky notes that you can move, sort, and rearrange. Other tools such as Notability and Evernote let you demonstrate digital note-taking techniques. These tools are great in the moment for how fast and easy they are to use. Sometimes they result in fleeting visual records, though, so consider if you want more permanent artifacts or if digital display is sufficient.

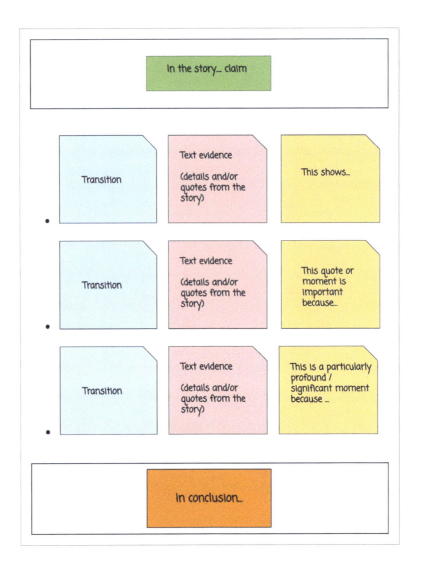

Curiosity, Inquisitiveness, and Immersion for Vocabulary Connections

As you embark on planned vocabulary instruction, yes, cohesion matters. Yes, collaborative planning is effective. *But in all of this,* trust your teacher instincts that nudge you to make room for collective curiosity to shape what happens in your classroom. Maybe you'll notice your students becoming enamored about collecting scientific vocabulary, and you'll find yourself unexpectedly teaching Latin names for plants or species. Maybe your classroom is full of multilingual learners and you all become obsessed with cognates and etymology, and you'll spend more time with AI, finding related words across languages, and histories of words from students' cultures. Maybe your morphology lessons lead some kids to want to start a Latin club. Or your critical literacy lessons on names and power lead children to critique their social studies text, leading to new book orders and lots of probing questions that merit investigation.

You are a teacher. That means you are a director, a producer, an author, a muse, a mentor, a humorist, a researcher, an instigator. As you turn the page to dig into all the lessons that follow, lean into your instincts. Adjust. Adapt. Embrace those teaching moments that engage and excite your students. Language is there for us to explore and revel in, and it's a wonder to watch a classroom of budding linguists make vocabulary connections on their own. Follow them!

Part I

Literary Vocabulary

Collecting Literary Vocabulary

The Scope of These Lessons— What's Going to Happen!

The lessons in this chapter engage students in collecting words to describe characters and their emotions. You'll begin with a digital narrative—a short, visually compelling story that draws in all learners. I suggest *Joy and Heron* but also include suggestions for other digital narratives and picture books to give you options for changing out the text to address a variety of grade-level needs. You won't worry about distinguishing between traits and emotions at the start, but instead will focus on how characters have many sides, and how readers see new sides as the story continues. You'll also emphasize that when talking about characters, the author doesn't usually give you the words that describe these characters. The author doesn't say "and so this shows, deep down, that Joy is **lonely**." Instead, it falls on readers to pay close attention to detail, and they think about what words best describe that character in the moment.

Learners will create their own word collections of traits and emotions, and they'll pause often to compare their words with a partner, explaining their thinking. You'll also create a class collection by charting the work children are doing—and you'll offer some direct instruction, teaching new words, and giving examples from the story to create meaning for learners. You'll be grouping words in semantic clusters (grouping words that are related in meaning together) as a way to foster children's contextual understanding and increase the likelihood that they will retain and use these words because they are attached to characters and stories they love (Hiebert, 2011, 2020; Hiebert and Pearson, 2013).

Anytime I am going to engage learners in close reading, I like to talk about the Ladder of Abstraction. This term was first coined many years ago by S.I. Hayakawa in his book *Language in Thought and Action* (1991). Hayakawa used the ladder to suggest how language shifts from concrete, observable phenomena to abstract, less tangible concepts. Later, in *Writing Tools: 55 Essential Strategies for Every Writer*, master writing teacher and journalist Roy Peter Clark returned to the Ladder of Abstraction, noting how we consistently move from details to ideas as we move up and down the ladder (Clark, 2016). That is, one partner may say, "Joy growls at Heron!" They are noting a detail. Their partner may reply, "Yes, Joy is **aggressive**!" further developing the idea. Together, they can collect more details to support that idea, or develop more ideas from that detail.

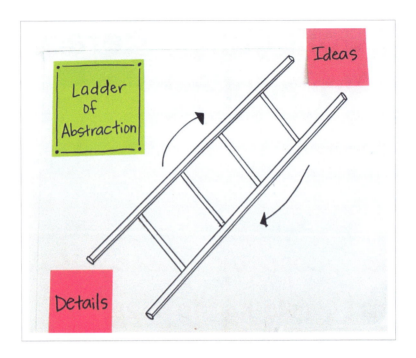

As you do this work, you'll plan explicit language goals for your multilingual learners, encouraging them to *collect in English* as a new language, to *translanguage* as they reach for literary words they know in their first language, and to *translate* as techniques for maximizing their full linguistic repertoires and developing literary vocabulary in all their languages (Espinosa and Ascenzi-Moreno, 2021; García et al., 2017; Kelly and Hou, 2022; Lake and Beisly, 2019). If you'd like to read more about explicit techniques for supporting and affirming multilingual learners, I suggest two books: *Literacy Foundations for English Learners: A Comprehensive Guide to Evidence-Based Instruction*, by Elsa Cárdenas-Hagan (2020), and *The Translanguaging Classroom*, by García et al. (2017).

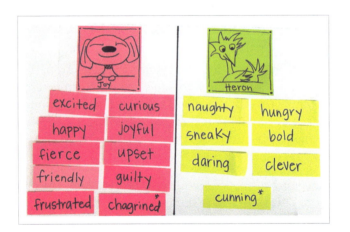

Finally, you'll offer extensions. You'll teach a variety of ways to deepen students' knowledge, such as organizing word groups into verticals by shades of meaning, sketching story mountains that track character change over time, and a variety of sorting exercises that lead to nuanced conversations about interpretation and increased usage. It's up to you if you also want to continue this work across new narratives, both digital and print, so that students transfer and apply the words they are using (I would!).

Learning Goals

Expect your learners to engage in intense oral language practice that increases usage very quickly. Expect your learners to see new relationships between words, and to learn a variety of new words. Expect your learners to develop nuanced ideas about characters in the stories they are reading, and to develop these ideas with more expressive language.

Here are some specific learning goals that are built into the lessons in this chapter.

- To swiftly and dramatically increase students' usage of literary vocabulary by linking word collections to ideas about beloved characters and stories.

- To forge connections between groups of words based on meaning.

- To explore shades of meanings inside of word groups.

- To increase opportunities for learners to transfer and apply expressive language as they explore new characters, new stories.

- To increase literary vocabulary in more than one language for multilingual learners.

- To foster a sense of joy, playfulness, and agency among vocabulary learners.

Text Recommendations

I suggest launching this work with an animated digital narrative (I demonstrate with *Joy and Heron*). These digital narratives tell compelling stories and are literally wordless. The multimodal quality of these narratives makes them engaging and inclusive (Ehrenworth, Gould, and Roman, 2025; Reyes-Torres and Portalés Raga, 2020; Zapata, 2022). All your learners will have things to say, and won't get caught up finding words in the story—instead they'll pay attention to detail, and infer from close reading. And, because these stories develop swiftly, learners collect a lot of words in one session. If you have time to repeat the lessons in Chapter 1 across a progression of texts, I suggest practicing this work on a few digital narratives at first, collecting lots of words, increasing usage, and generating a lot of text-based conversation. Then move to picture books, so that your learners can still find secrets in the illustrations, as they also learn about characters from the things they say and do. Meanwhile, encourage students to transfer this work to the other texts they are reading for class, which might include independent reading, book clubs, or all-class shared books.

Here are a few favorite digital narratives that make these lessons especially engaging and rewarding. Check out the website www.vocabularyconnections.org to find more:

Joy and Heron

Pip

Dust Bunnies

Piper (short version)

L.O.U.

Hair Love

Supporting Act

Opportunities for Transfer and Application

Your learners will collect and use a lot of literary vocabulary in these lessons. If you want to increase transfer, invite them to continue this work in their independent reading books, book club books, or all-class shared texts, depending on what students are reading in your literacy curriculum. The beautiful thing about this work is that it is immediately transferable, it provides a lean form of jotting, and it leads to nuanced, text-based conversations. You may want to create an anchor chart to document the strategies you teach, across these lessons, as a cueing system for transfer.

An anchor chart helps learners remember and transfer skills and habits

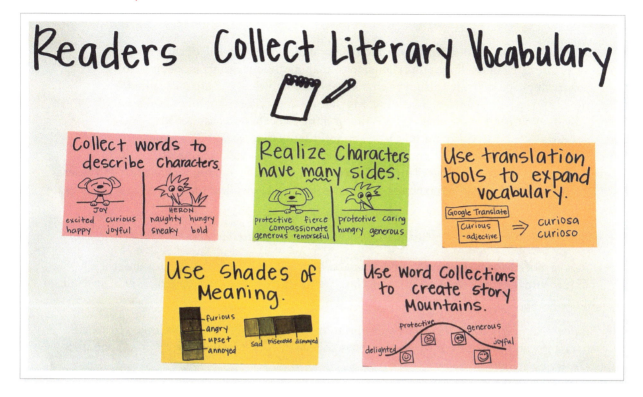

Video clubs or digital narrative clubs can be magical opportunities for transfer. Each club needs one device, and they take charge of duplicating the work the class did with *Joy and Heron*. They collect words to describe the character(s), they explore secret sides of characters, they use their verticals to have nuanced conversations about characters' traits and feelings, and so on. The work is accessible and joyful and leads to new collections of literary vocabulary. It builds on the work of Reyes-Torres and Portalés Raga (2020), focusing on multiliteracies and interpretation of multimodal texts as pathways to deep interpretation and close reading. Readers also do a lot of comparing and contrasting of characters, as they think about how Piper is like or unlike Joy or what new verticals a character suggests.

You can also continue with this work in shared texts or book clubs, creating an opportunity to deepen the work students are doing in those texts. Book clubs, especially, benefit from the lean jotting children engage in, and the literary conversations the work launches. Collecting literary vocabulary fits beautifully with:

- character studies
- book clubs
- literary essays
- test prep
- intervention groups
- enrichment groups

Assessment Options

We know that the breadth and depth of students' vocabulary supports all of their academic prowess, from reading comprehension to making their writing compelling, to their spoken language skills. It's also true that vocabulary knowledge is unconstrained, as in, there is no specific, contained set of words that we are trying to instill in learners. I especially like Margaret McKeown's (2015) discussion of vocabulary assessment, where she speaks extensively about how it is not definitions that we should assess, but how learners use words contextually. Ultimately, literary vocabulary acquisition is multidimensional, content dependent, and develops continually, making it challenging to assess in formal, meaningful ways. Nevertheless, you and your students will want to monitor and celebrate growth.

Some possibilities for assessment (including self-assessment) include:

- *Literary conversations.* Listen to or record partners talking about characters in the story, as they point to and use their word collections. Note students' fluency with applying Tier 2, specialized words.

- *Students' word collections.* Note the appropriateness of words learners have linked to specific characters, and the kinds of words they have collected (for example, Tier 2 words, cognates, translating across languages).

- *Notebook entries.* Ask students to generate a notebook entry that analyzes a character, and that incorporates some of the literary vocabulary they think is most important in describing that character.

- *Literary essays.* Evaluate how students incorporate literary vocabulary in their formal writing, such as literary essays. Notice how more nuanced vocabulary supports nuanced interpretation.

Links to Standards

Reading Anchor Standard 1: Read closely to determine what the text says explicitly/implicitly and make logical inferences from it; cite specific textual evidence when writing or speaking to support conclusions drawn from the text.

Reading Anchor Standard 4: Interpret words and phrases as they are used in a text, including determining technical, connotative, and figurative meanings, and analyze how specific word choices shape meaning or tone.

Reading Anchor Standard 5: Analyze the structure of texts.

Reading Anchor Standard 7: Integrate and evaluate content presented in diverse media and formats.

Reading Language Anchor Standard 5: Demonstrate understanding of figurative language, word relationships, and nuances in word meanings.

Writing Anchor Standard 5: Draw evidence from literary or informational texts to support analysis, reflection, and research.

Speaking and Listening Anchor Standard 1: Prepare for and participate effectively in a range of conversations and collaborations with diverse partners.

Speaking and Listening Anchor Standard 6: Adapt speech to a variety of contexts and communicative tasks, demonstrating command of academic English when indicated or appropriate.

Language Anchor Standard 6: Acquire and accurately use general academic and content-specific words and phrases sufficient for reading, writing, speaking, and listening; demonstrate independence in gathering and applying vocabulary knowledge when considering a word or phrase important to comprehension or expression.

Lesson 1.1

Describing Characters

Considerations

Lesson summary: In this session you will launch the work of collecting literary vocabulary by gathering words to describe characters. You won't worry, at this point, about whether these words identify traits or emotions—that work will come later. You will suggest that children work with a partner to come up with words to describe two characters from a lively, engaging story, *Joy and Heron*, and you'll create a shared class word collection. You'll watch only the first half of the video today—1 minute and 53 seconds. You're also beginning to democratize this vocabulary acquisition. For example, some learners might not come up with the word **sneaky**, or the word **daring**, but once they hear these words explained, they'll use these words, continuing to find examples in the story.

This work introduces children to the notion of literary vocabulary, and supports them in gathering wide collections of words to describe characters they love. They will also learn new words.

Estimated lesson time: 12 minutes.

Materials and preparation: Prepare a chart, either on chart paper or using a notebook page that you can display, with the labels "Joy" and "Heron," and colored sticky notes underneath. You may visit www.vocabularyconnections.org to see examples of word collections for *Joy and Heron*.

You'll need chart paper and medium-size sticky notes in two colors, or a notebook page and small sticky notes to display—this will house the class word collection, generated across the lesson. Learners need their own paper and sticky notes to collect words. They can also use a collection of note cards, with an envelope or baggy for storage.

Additional lesson options: If you have time for an extended read-aloud session, you can combine Lesson 1 with Lesson 2, and watch the entire narrative, collecting words across the whole arc of the story. The time for the combined lesson then is about 20 minutes.

Launching the Lesson

Introduce the big work of increasing children's literary vocabulary (and developing their close reading skills) by collecting words to describe characters. Give a couple of tips. Then introduce the characters in the story. Also model a way to take notes/collect words.

For example, you might say, "Readers, I want to give you a couple of tips as you start this work. The first tip is—in the kinds of stories you are reading now, characters are complicated. That means you'll need to collect lots of words to describe them. And second, the author is never going to say, 'and so this shows that deep down, Pip was **lonely**.' Instead, you have to pay close attention to detail, including tiny details like changes in characters' expressions. Essentially, you are moving up and down a Ladder of Abstraction, sometimes noticing details, and coming up with ideas from these details, and sometimes finding details to support your ideas."

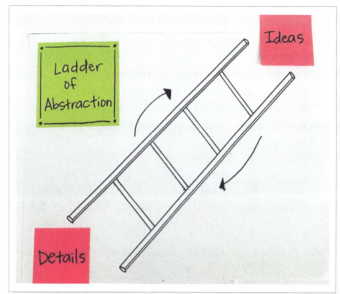

You might also introduce the text, saying, "The main characters in this story are Joy, a puppy who is going fishing with her owner, and Heron, a bird who visits the fishing boat." Point to where you've jotted "Joy" and "Heron" and to the sketches of their pictures, so as you say these characters' names in the lessons, learners get to know these characters.

Engagement: Collecting Words and Oral Language Practice

Start the digital read-aloud of *Joy and Heron*, voicing over to help students get started, then pausing for partners to share. Make a visual collection of vocabulary for the whole class as an example. You may also offer a word or two to the collection. Play the first 30 seconds.

For example, after just a few seconds of the video, when Joy has jumped onto the boat with such glee, you might say, "You should have some words to describe Joy already! I'm thinking, for example … **excited**! Jot a couple of words and then share with your partner."

As children share, collect some of their words, and show your chart/demonstration notebook page. Each time you say a word, give an example from the story of when Joy acted that way. For example, you might say, "some of you said that Joy seemed very **joyful**, when she jumps in the air and leaps into the boat with so much energy."

Continue to play the video, right up to the moment when Heron flies off after the fight but before she flies to the nest (you'll finish it in Lesson 2). Then invite partners to share their words with each other and add to your class collection of words to describe the characters—your page now functions as the class collection.

You can "call in" individual children by summarizing and elevating what they say. For example, you might say, "Amber suggested that Heron is **sneaky**! That's a great word, let's add that. Heron is **sneaky**! He arrives when the fisherman isn't looking, and he gets Joy in trouble!"

Offer direct instruction, teaching students a couple of new words.

Teach children a couple of new, sophisticated words. It's often helpful to teach words that combine words learners already know. For example, you might say, "I want to teach you a new word for Joy. It's **chagrined**. When someone feels **guilty** but also kind of **upset**, especially if they are unfairly **accused**, like Joy does when her owner speaks sharply to her, the word for that is **chagrined**!"

You might also say, "I want to teach you another new word. When someone is **clever** and **sneaky**, a fancy word for that is **cunning**. Like when Heron sneaks up slowly, waiting until the fisherman's back is turned to grab the worms, she is so **cunning**!"

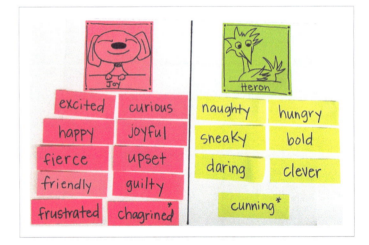

Support your multilingual learners (and all learners) in translanguaging and translating, and in exploring cognates.

You might say, "You can use all your languages as you do this work. If you know a fancy literary vocabulary word, for example, in Spanish, jot it down in Spanish, and then you can work on translating that word into English. You can use an app like Google Translate to find the translation, and write the word in both languages. Keep a lookout for words that sound the same in more than one language. These words are called 'cognates,' and they help you to learn lots of new words, simply by recognizing similarities to words you already know in one language."

Application

Compliment students as linguists. Encourage children to use these strategies to collect new vocabulary whenever they think about characters. Find a place on the wall where you can keep the class word collection, and have children save their own collections.

You might say, "I'm going to call you **linguists** now! **Linguists** are people who love words—and look at all the literary vocabulary words you've collected. I'm going to keep our class collection here on the wall, so we can return to it tomorrow. You keep your collections too. Remember, whenever you are building ideas about characters, one way you can do that work is to collect a lot of words, talk about them, develop ideas about characters. As you are reading other stories, think about the words you would use to describe the characters in those stories as well—you can reach for literary vocabulary whenever you are jotting about characters."

The work students will create during and after the lesson might look like ...

Notebook pages

Note card collection

Translanguaging collection

Cognate collection

Lesson 1.2

New Sides, New Words

Considerations

Lesson summary: In this session you will teach that characters often reveal new sides of themselves across a story, and readers find new words to describe these secret sides. You'll watch the rest of *Joy and Heron*, and you and your students will collect more words to describe the characters. This work deepens learners' usage of literary vocabulary as they review and extend their collections and use these words in discussions about the characters. It also deepens their insight into complex characters and how they reveal new sides of themselves across a narrative.

Estimated lesson time: 12 minutes.

Materials and preparation: You'll need the chart of words you collected in Lesson 1, which you'll add to.

Learners need their word collections that they started in Lesson 1.1. They should work with the same partner from Lesson 1.1.

Additional lesson options: You might pull a small group of multilingual learners who speak Romance languages such as Spanish, Italian, French, Portuguese (and allies who like to learn new languages) to especially explore cognates. Or you might pull some multilingual learners and allies to explore translation apps such as Google Translate or DeepL, so that they can instantly translate words they know in one language into English and vice versa—especially in classrooms where a student who is learning English as a new language needs an ally and there isn't another student who shares their first language. A digitally adept student can act as a powerful ally, especially when they are interested in learning words in new languages as well. Tomorrow's session teaches about translation apps, and you can set up the session with tech adept students by pulling a small group today, thus setting specific students up to play a strong role.

Launching the Lesson

Remind learners of the work they did in Lesson 1, of collecting words to describe Joy and Heron. Invite students to review their words and explain what happened in the story that supports their ideas. Then suggest that characters also reveal new, secret sides of themselves across a story, so readers need to prepare themselves to find new words to describe these sides.

You might say, "Linguists, you found so many words to describe Joy and Heron. Find your word collections. Tell your partner what you've learned so far about Joy and Heron. And partners, if your partner says a good idea, like 'Joy turned out to be **fierce**!' Don't just nod. Ask, 'what in the story makes you say that?' Ask for text evidence!"

You can increase your students' familiarity with new words by saying them out loud often and giving examples. For instance, you might say, "Oh, yes, and you learned the word **cunning**! Heron was so cunning, when she moved so **sneakily** and **cleverly** to steal the worm behind the fisherman's back!"

If any of your multilingual learners noticed cognates in yesterday's lesson, you can call attention to these words as well, saying something like, "And some of you noticed cognates—those are words that sound the same in different languages. Like in English, Joy is **fierce**, and in Spanish she is **feroz**!"

To introduce the upcoming work, you might say, "Readers, in the kinds of stories you are reading now, characters also have secret sides, parts of themselves that you only learn about later in the story. That is definitely going to happen in this story. Set your notes up so you're ready to collect new words to describe both Joy and Heron. I'm going to add some blank sticky notes to my collection, so I'm ready to jot when I discover new, secret sides."

Engagement: Collecting Words and Oral Language Practice

Play the beginning of the video again, or skim it. Then play the rest of the video, encouraging learners to collect new words, occasionally voicing over with your own ideas to model and increase engagement.

Reviewing the previous lesson's text and the literary words they've collected provides more opportunities for review. You might say, pointing to words in your collection, "Let's reread for a moment … oh, look how **excited** and **curious** Joy is at the start. And Joy seems **friendly** when Heron first arrives. Oh, but then when Heron is so **sneaky** and **naughty**, so **cunning**, Joy becomes **upset** and **protective**! Boy, does Heron seem **hungry**—in fact, we might say she seems **famished**, which means really, really **hungry**! She really wants these worms. Look how **fierce** Joy and Heron are as they fight over the worms."

Young readers pay more attention when you set them up with lenses for close reading. You might say, "Readers, remember how we said that some characters have secret sides, that you find out new things about them? Well sometimes that's because a character changes—something happens in the story that changes them. And other times, the character doesn't change; instead, the reader's thinking changes. Let's see what happens now. What new ideas do you have about Joy and Heron? Be ready to jot!"

As you play the video, you can voice over a bit, to support your learners. It might sound like, "Oh my gosh, wait a second, let's watch that again. Is it that Heron isn't **hungry**, it's that her children are hungry, and they can't eat fish—they need worms?! I feel like I misjudged Heron is **desperate**! Oh, Joy is looking the same way, she looks pretty **sad** …"

Invite partners to share. After they share, offer direct instruction—teach two new words, remorseful and compassionate.

As partners share their words, you can add to the class collection. Call children in as learners by giving them authorship for new words. "Alicia and Sara are suggesting that Joy feels **guilty** about not sharing the worms with Heron. And Juan and Sam are saying that both Joy and Heron are **generous** when they share first worms and then fish with each other! These are precise, literary words."

You might also say, "I want to teach you another new word. It's **remorseful**. When someone feels **sad** and a little **guilty**, like when Joy realizes that Heron wanted the worms to feed her hungry children, she feels **remorseful**. And another new word is **compassionate**. When someone is especially **kind**—and they commit acts of kindness, like when Joy shares the worms with Heron, we say they are **compassionate**."

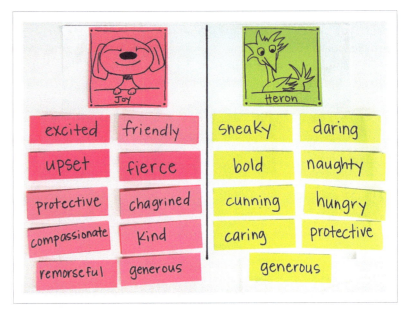

As students work, celebrate your multilingual learners (and all learners) for translanguaging and translating, and for exploring cognates. Demonstrate how you strive to learn words in new languages from your multilingual learners.

You might say, "I just learned that the Spanish word for **generous** is **generoso**, and the French word is **généreux**! And Ivanna just taught me that the Ukrainian word is **щедрий**."

Application

Summarize the work children did of collecting new words to describe new sides of characters. Encourage them to keep their word collections, and to continue this work as they read other stories. Also encourage them to use their new words in new situations.

Depending on what work you are doing in your reading curriculum, you can create immediate opportunities for transfer. For instance, if students are engaged in independent reading or book clubs, you might say, "Take this work to the stories you are reading! Ask yourself—how are the main characters in your story like Joy or Heron? Are they **cunning**, or **remorseful**, or **compassionate**?"

Or you can encourage learners to use these words in their conversations with friends and family. You might say, "Keep your word collections, linguists! But more importantly, try to use some of these words today and tonight. If you watch a television show, think about what words you can describe the characters with. Surprise your family by saying you are **famished**, or thank a friend for being **compassionate**. If you speak more than one language, teach a friend or family member some of your new words. Every time you use one of these words, you are lodging it solidly in your long-term memory, where it will be there, waiting for you to use it again, brilliantly."

The work students will create during and after the lesson might look like ...

Bilingual learners collect literary vocabulary in both their languages

Some students prefer to create digital collections

Vocabulario para el vídeo, *Joy y Heron*

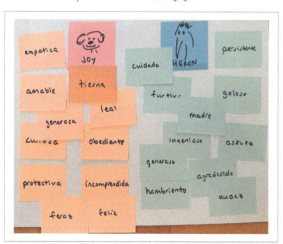

This club collected words to describe characters in the digital narrative, *L.O.U.*

This club collects words to describe the character Piper, from the video *Piper*

Another club member organizes words in different colors as new sides of Piper are revealed

Lesson **1.3**

Translation and Alliances

Considerations

Lesson summary: In this session you will teach students that in this global multilingual world people speak and write many languages, and that learners can begin to learn vocabulary in multiple languages from each other. You'll suggest that learners can use translation apps to teach each other new words, and you'll introduce a couple of translation tools. This work doesn't just break down language barriers. It opens doors to cultural understandings, enriches classroom interactions, and builds language learning alliances.

Estimated lesson time: 15 minutes.

Materials and preparation: You'll need the chart of words you collected in Lesson 1 and 2.

You and your students need access to a few digital devices that will provide translation apps such as:

Google Translate (for laptops, phones, iPads)

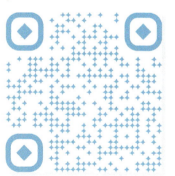

iTranslate (for phones and iPads)

DeepL Translate (for laptops, phones, iPads)

I like to offer two or three choices of translation tools, so that children learn *they* can find and explore translation apps, including new ones that will become available. Of course, you can choose one with your class. Most translation apps are intuitive, and most children dive into technology fearlessly. Expect to have to teach less than you'd anticipate about how to use translation tools.

Learners need their word collections that they started in Lesson 1.1 and 1.2. They should work in small language-based interest groups. As in, if a few children speak Spanish, they can work with a few children who would like to learn some Spanish words. If some children would like to learn words in a language that is new in the class, they can gather at a table to learn words in that new language. You might have place mats at tables, with language invitations.

Additional lesson options: Some languages, such as Romance languages, will especially reward cognate study. You might pull a small group of students who are working across these languages to especially collect cognates. Other languages involve masculine or feminine adjectives. You might pull a small group and show how, if you decide that Joy is female, then the Spanish adjectives will mostly end in a, for example.

Launching the Lesson

Describe the significance of crossing language barriers and building cultural bridges, and the role that translation tools can play. Divide students into language-interest groups or let them divide themselves.

You might say, "Linguists, we live in this complex and beautiful world, where people speak and write many languages. And we're lucky enough to have two resources to help us cross language barriers. We have each other—some of you speak multiple languages. And we have translation tools. We don't have to be limited by the words we already know—we can begin to learn words in lots of languages!"

To affirm students' linguistic assets, you might say, "Today, we are going to learn how to talk about Joy and Heron in more than one language! You'll gather in interest groups at tables, and use translation tools to learn new words, including how to pronounce them. If you are already studying Spanish as well as English, you might join a Spanish-English table. Or if you are really good at technology, you can host a table that wants to learn a language that is new in our classroom. Get yourselves divided into some language groups now (or go to the table that has your name on it)."

Engagement: Translating and Trying out Words

Demonstrate how to explore translation tools, inviting children to use their ingenuity to figure out which tool they like, how to translate words, and how to learn pronunciation. Invite children to translate their favorite words and record them in their notes.

To demonstrate how you explore one tool, such as Google Translate, instead of giving a "how-to," which will set you up for a future in which many children ask for directions continually, demonstrate how to explore a tool. You might say, "I wonder how this works? It looks like it has a feature that lets me set what language I want to speak or write in, and what I want to translate to. It also looks like it has a little volume button that gives pronunciation, that's useful."

You might visit with the Spanish-English group to alert them to masculine and feminine endings. You might say, "Some languages, like Spanish, have masculine and feminine endings. So, if you decide Joy is female, then you'll need female endings, which are mostly 'a.' To get a translation app to give you female endings, you can see if the app provides choices of gender and endings, or you can type 'she is **protective**' and it will give you 'es **protectora**.'"

You might also talk about gender neutrality in language. You might say, "English adjectives don't assign gender. But pronouns such as *she* or *he* do. We've said *she* for Joy, but we're not sure. In English, people can use *they* when they don't know how someone identifies."

Translation apps will often offer choices of gendered word endings

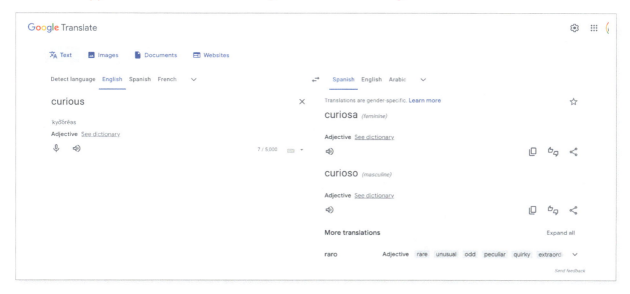

As children work, voice over new words, to create a sense of shared learning and celebration. "I love this word **persistent**—in Spanish it's **persistente**. And look how beautiful it is when spelled in Korean—영구!"

Application

To wrap up, invite children to teach learners at another table a word that applies to Joy or Heron in a new language—what the word means, how to write it, how to pronounce it. Encourage them to begin to keep word collections in more than one language, and to move through the world with an eagerness to cross language barriers.

You might send an ambassador partnership from each table to another table to teach a new word. It might sound like, "Linguists, you've learned so many new words, in many languages! If the whole world were like you, we would all be able to communicate freely. Let's have you each teach someone a word that describes Joy or Heron in a new language. Get together with a partner. Decide on a word you'll teach. Write it, say it, and when you're ready, half of you are going to switch to other tables, to teach new words, and learn new words."

The work students will create during and after the lesson might look like ...

Using DeepL to translate

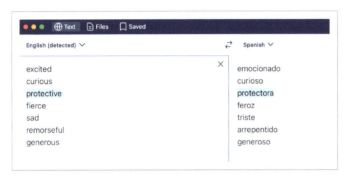

Celebrating children's linguistic diversity and competencies

Lesson 1.4

Shades of Meaning

Considerations

Lesson summary: In this session you will introduce verticals—collections of adjectives that are grouped by meaning, and arranged by intensity. For example, **annoyed-frustrated-angry-furious**. You'll provide students with starter sets for verticals, and invite them to do three things:

1. add to the verticals with other words they know

2. discuss *Joy and Heron* and when and why a specific word describes that character

3. create other verticals for words they need to describe the characters

This work helps students begin to acquire more literary vocabulary by becoming familiar with semantic clusters. It also helps them begin to sort out shades of meaning for words that mean somewhat, but not exactly, the same thing. Using verticals also helps children express more nuanced interpretations about characters.

Estimated lesson time: 12 minutes.

Materials and preparation: You'll provide a collection of verticals for the most essential character descriptors, anchored with Tier 1 words such as **mad, sad, happy, scared, nice, mean**. You may create these with sticky notes, as paint swatch cards from the hardware store, as printed colored lists, or as cards in an envelope that children may sort. Most children benefit from a starter set, as they won't know all the words in a vertical. It's helpful to post verticals on a classroom vocabulary wall and for children to have their own sets on hand during read-aloud and any reading experience. Visit the website www.vocabularyconnections.org to download sample verticals for *Joy and Heron*.

Additional lesson options: An optional extension is to engage students in flash debates, where they choose a word and defend why it is the most precise word to describe the character. For instance, is Joy **annoyed** or **furious** the first time Heron steals the worm? How do you know?

Launching the Lesson

Introduce the notion of verticals and explain how verticals help us learn more words and explore shades of meaning. Give an example—demonstrate how you might argue on behalf of Joy being annoyed or furious at different moments in the story.

33

Children like verticals and grasp them quickly. It can be helpful to show a visual such as a thermometer or speedometer or volume indicator or paint color sample.

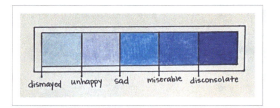

You might say, "Today you're going to explore shades of meanings, working on making your literary vocabulary very precise. To do that, you'll use verticals, which are collections of words that are grouped by meaning. The words at the bottom will be the least intense, as the words toward the top become more intense. You can also arrange words as a speedometer, or like a volume control, with the emotion getting louder. And you can color verticals with darker shades, to show intensity."

Then you might demonstrate, saying, "Verticals help us be more precise—so you can argue on behalf of a precise word. For instance, I think I'd say that when Heron first appears on the boat and steals a worm, Joy is annoyed, which means a little bit mad. But by the third time she steals a worm, Joy is furious, which means so mad you can't control your emotions!"

Engagement—Oral Language Practice with Verticals

Invite students to review the verticals you've provided for them, and to add any words they know to the verticals. Then set them up with a partner to defend why a word on the vertical describes Joy and Heron in a specific moment in the story.

You might say, "Begin by previewing the verticals and talking about the words you know. You can add to a vertical, as well, with sticky notes. If you want to create a vertical yourself, I have some cards, and you can jot words and sort them by intensity with your partner."

enraged	inconsolable	petrified
furious	desolate	terrified
angry/mad	miserable	frightened
upset	unhappy/sad	scared
frustrated	downhearted	timid
annoyed	dejected	nervous
joyful	malevolent	compassionate
delighted	pitiless	empathetic
happy	vicious	kind/nice
content	malicious	sympathetic
cheerful	cruel/mean	thoughtful
pleased	spiteful	pleasant

To launch literary conversations, you might say, "You heard me defend the idea that Joy started out **annoyed** and became **furious**. Try that work out. Pick a word you think is precisely right for describing Joy or Heron in a specific moment in the story. Explain to your partner why that word fits—and defend your idea with details from the story."

Application

Suggest that students use these verticals whenever they are talking about characters. Also suggest that they can create new verticals, or ask for new ones, when they think they need a new word group. Post verticals on a vocabulary wall.

You might say, "Let's keep these verticals on hand for read-aloud, and anytime you are having a discussion about a story—you'll especially want them for book club talks and literary essays. Linguists, verticals will help you be more precise, and they help you learn many new words. Keep yours near you as you read, write, and talk about stories. Make new ones. Ask for new ones if you need a new word collection. Like maybe the character in your story is **proud**. But you can ask yourself: is she a little proud, like **confident**, or is she over-the-top proud, like **arrogant**? I'll keep verticals on the wall to help our discussions, and you keep your verticals on hand whenever you are reading and writing."

The work students will create during the lesson might look like ...

Children add to classroom verticals

Minicharts support readers' vocabulary

- Enraged
- Furious
- Angry
- Upset
- Annoyed

- Compassionate
- Generous
- Kind
- Thoughtful
- Nice

- Joyful
- Delighted
- Content
- Happy
- Cheerful

- Despairing
- Miserable
- Sad
- Discontent
- Dejected

Paint strips make useful bookmarks for collecting shades of meaning

Speedometers can help learners visualize intensity

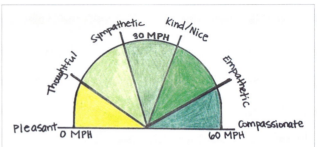

Verticales en español

Kids make verticals in their book clubs

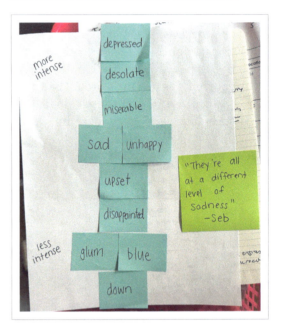

Lesson 1.5

Story Mountains

Considerations

Lesson summary: In this session you'll invite your budding linguists to return to their word collections and sort them in a new way—along a story mountain. As learners choose words that match moments in the story, they have new opportunities to use their literary vocabulary in context and to explain how details in the story support their thinking. Students will also sketch a story mountain, and they'll move sticky notes from their word collection to this story mountain, choosing words to describe Joy across the story. Or, if they made their word collections with cards, today they may want to jot on sticky notes.

This work deepens oral language practice and creates opportunities for deeper contextual understanding of literary vocabulary. It also helps readers to attend to details in the text that suggest how characters often change across a narrative.

Estimated lesson time: 12 minutes.

Materials and preparation: You'll need to sketch, or have already prepared, a story mountain of *Joy and Heron*. It's helpful for your multilingual learners if you include small sketches of the moments in the story. You'll also need sticky notes to add character descriptors for Joy to the story mountain. You can use the sticky notes you jotted in Lesson 1 and 2, or have a new set on hand just for this lesson (if you don't want to disrupt that chart). It's also helpful to have the verticals from Lesson 4 on hand. Visit the website www.vocabularyconnections.org to download sample verticals and a story mountain.

Additional lesson options: Alongside supporting vocabulary acquisition and character interpretation, this work also supports part-to-whole work (much assessed on ELA exams). Students can use their story mountains as a kind of game board. One partner can hold up a sticky note, with **furious** or **remorseful** on it, for example, and the other partner has to decide where it goes.

Launching the Lesson

Review your word collections and verticals for *Joy and Heron*, and have students do the same. Then invite students to sketch a story mountain for *Joy and Heron*, as you also create one. You might skim the video, without sound, to remind students of important moments.

37

Because every opportunity to talk about their word collections provides oral language practice, it's helpful to begin by inviting learners to review their words. You might say, "Linguists, have your word collections and verticals for Joy and Heron in front of you. As you review them, use this precise vocabulary to tell your partner what you learned about Joy and Heron across the story. When did the characters surprise you? What new sides of themselves did they reveal? Use your literary words!"

Sketching their own story mountain helps students think over the events and structure of the story, which will help them assign character descriptors to each part. You might say, "Now we're going to do something new. We're going to sketch a story mountain, and label it with the big moments in the story. Leave room on top of your mountain for sticky notes, because we'll be doing more with these sketches in a second. Review with your partner what happened in the story, and capture these moments on our story mountains." Then you can fast fast-forward through the narrative, pausing on big moments to add them to your story mountain.

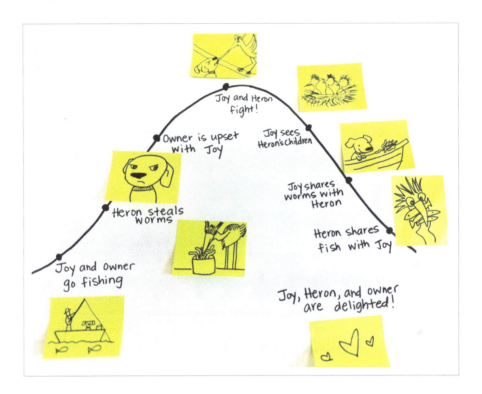

Engagement—Sorting and Explaining

Briefly demonstrate how you choose a word that matches a specific part of the story, and explain why that word fits a word to describe Joy. Then invite students to work together in partnerships to label their story mountains with words to describe Joy. Encourage learners to support their thinking with details from the story. Also encourage them to turn to their verticals to choose precise vocabulary.

You might say, "Now, watch as I try this work out. I'm looking at this first moment in the story, when Joy is getting on the boat. She seems so **happy** and **excited**. Hmm, let me look at the vertical for **happy**. I think I might say, actually, that Joy is **delighted**! The way Joy bounces, and leaps in the air, and her ears are up, and she seems to be smiling—yes, that says to me that Joy is delighted!" I'll put that sticky note here.

Unpack the steps you followed, and invite students to continue. You might say, "Do you see how I thought about what was happening in that moment of the story, and what word best describes Joy in that moment? And I looked at one of my verticals, too, to see if there was a precise word I might want to use. Then I explained my thinking. You can do this too. Go on with the rest of the story mountain. Work with your partner. Use your word collections and verticals to choose precise words to describe Joy, and explain your thinking to each other as you annotate your story mountain."

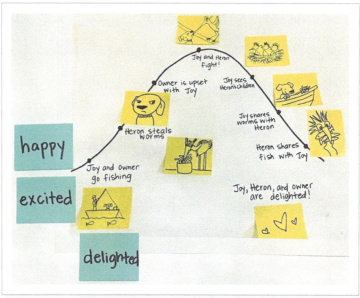

As always, encourage your multilingual learners to use all their linguistic assets as they tackle this work. You might say, "All of you who are learning more than one language, remember that you can use all your languages as you tackle this work. Remember the translation tools you have on hand, and strive to reach for the just-right-precise word you want!"

Application

Suggest to students that this work of tracing character change is smart thinking work to do whenever they are reading, and especially if they are in book clubs, shared texts, or thinking about literary essays. Share that not all stories are structured along a simple mountain, and share a simple sketch that shows other ways stories might go.

Tracing character change is always smart thinking to do in a story. You might say, "Readers, it's not just Joy who changes across a story. Most characters do. You can try this work out in any text that you are reading, especially one you are going to talk and write about with others."

It's helpful to show readers different ways stories can be structured, so their sketches can be more flexible. You might say, "I do want to give you one tip. Not all stories are problem-solution—they're not all structured along a mountain like this. Some stories have multiple peaks, multiple moments of tension. Some stories tend to go downward: things start out okay for the main character, then they descend into a kind of dark pit of trouble, and then eventually the character begins to climb out of the pit. And some stories are circular: they start and end in similar spaces. You can sketch a story map in any of those ways, and then trace character change across the map."

The work students will create during and after the lesson might look like ...

Readers make a story mountain for Joy

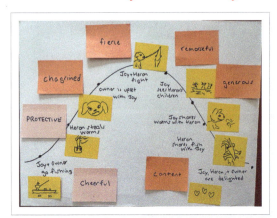

This reader traces a circular story path for her main character, Pip

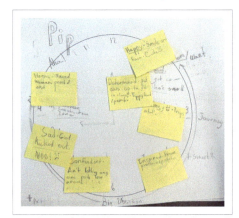

This reader creates a story mountain in Spanish for Joy

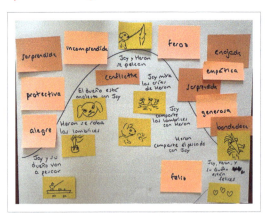

Partners create a story mountain for *Pip*

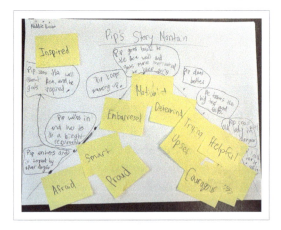

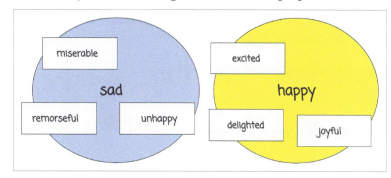

Lesson 1.6 Word Games

Considerations

Lesson summary: In this session you'll teach students three word games that will deepen their engagement with literary vocabulary. You'll teach:

- semantic word sorts
- Venn diagrams for sorting overlapping character traits and emotions
- word equations for creating new words

You can set these up as centers, which children rotate through, or demonstrate them in a lesson and invite partners to play the game of their choice today.

This work increases students' proficiency with literary vocabulary, their agency with seeing relationships between words, and their engagement with words.

Estimated lesson time: 15 minutes.

Materials and preparation: You'll need paper and markers for you and the children to sketch Venn diagrams. Children also often like crayons or colored pencils to shade parts of their diagrams. For the word sort game, you'll need to print and cut up lists of words, put them into baggies (I usually combine two lists per baggie, to match word sort place mats, which each have two word circles per mat). Sometimes stopwatches make games more fun for (some, not all) kids, and you can have these on hand as well. Visit the website www.vocabularyconnections.org to download sample placemats and words lists.

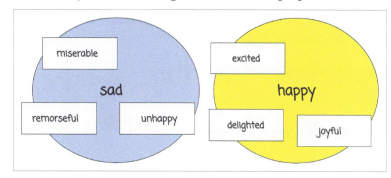

Additional lesson options: You might decide to introduce each of these games in its own lesson. In that case, I would introduce the word sorts either right after verticals—Lesson 1.4, or as the first of these games. I would introduce Venn diagrams for shared traits and emotions right after Secret Sides—Lesson 1.2, or as the second of these games. I would introduce word equations to create new words as the final and hardest of the games. Another game option for multilingual learners who speak Romance languages is finding cognates. You can use the same word lists for the word sorts, and invite learners to jot as many cognates as they can.

Launching the Lesson

Give a micro-demonstration of each game so that learners know how to play.

For the word sort, you might say: "Word collectors! Today you have three centers you can rotate through. Each center has a word game that you can play with a partner. The first center is a word sort, and it leans on the work you did with verticals—but there are even more words here! For this game, you try to sort words into their circles by meaning. You'll know some of the words, and for others you'll need to lean on each other. You can use any tools, like translation tools or dictionaries. You may not complete all the sorts today."

For the Venn diagrams to sort overlapping traits and emotions, you might say, "In *Joy and Heron*, and the stories you are reading, sometimes characters have overlapping traits and emotions. In this game, you'll sketch and color Venn diagrams. One circle will represent Joy, and another will represent Heron—you can decide what colors represent each character. Then you'll sort which traits and emotions are only for one character, and which overlap."

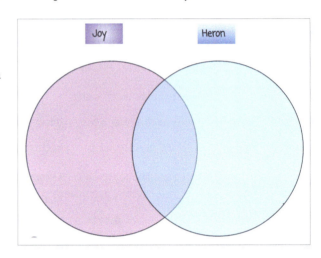

For the word equations to create new words, you might say, "The final game is tricky. In this game, you'll combine word meanings to create new words. For example, when someone is **clever** plus **sneaky**, we say they are **cunning**. Heron is **cunning** when she steals the worms behind the fisherman's back! When someone feels **sad** plus **guilty**, like Joy does when she sees Heron's hungry babies, we say they feel **remorseful**. You'll think of others, and you can use your imagination—like maybe **scared** plus **brave** equals **heroic**! Or you can go the other way. You can take **brave** minus **scared** and equal **fearless**! You can use your verticals to help you find some starter words."

$$\textbf{brave} - \textbf{scared} = \textbf{fearless}$$
$$\textbf{clever} + \textbf{sneaky} = \textbf{cunning}$$

Engagement—Sorting, Creating, Collaborating with Words

Encourage children to use all their word knowledge, and to lean on digital tools such as translation tools and dictionaries as game helpers. Timers can make a game more exciting for those who enjoy time trials.

Some kids love the excitement of a time trial. For these players, you can set up timers, and you might say, "Players, you have three minutes to sort as many words as possible! Five, four, three, two, one ... go!" Or you can set up a partner as a timekeeper for a game. A feeling of being rushed is NOT exhilarating for all students, so keep this optional, as it can cause other students to feel pressured and nervous.

For multilingual learners, remind them they can use their translation tools. They might jot translations on the back of their word cards as they sort. They might write word equations in more than one language. It might sound like, "Learners of many languages, remember you can use your translation tools! You can also create Venn diagrams and word equations in more than one language. We're here to get stronger in all our languages!"

Application

Encourage children to return to these games in and out of school. You might make them available during choice time, for example. You can also invite children to become game-makers, inviting them to invent new word games to deepen literary vocabulary.

Remember that children retain literary vocabulary more when they associate it with characters and stories they love. In encouraging learners to go on with these games, you might say, "Vocabulary gamers! You did some great word sorts and equations today. We had some exciting time trials. Most importantly, you deepened your word knowledge. I'll make these games available during choice time."

Then you might add, "But ask yourself: When else could you play these games with literary vocabulary? When would it make sense, for example, to sketch overlapping character traits and emotions? What other stories could you play these games with?"

And finally, you might issue an invitation. "Some of you are really good at games, and you may have new ideas for new games. If you think of a game you could play that will deepen your literary vocabulary, let me know. You can print word collections, you can design something on the computer—use your imaginations, game-makers!"

The work students will create during and after the lesson might look like ...

Overlapping traits and emotions

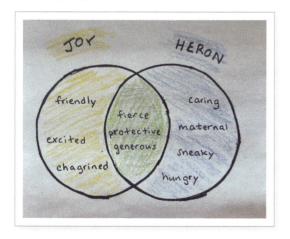

Word sorts

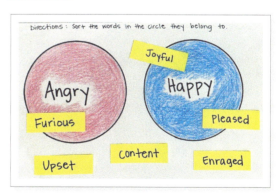

Word equations

A Venn diagram for word combinations

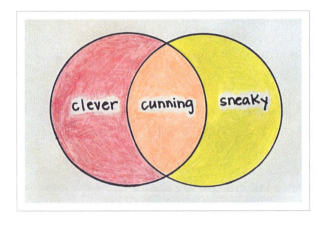

An anchor chart helps learners remember and transfer skills and habits

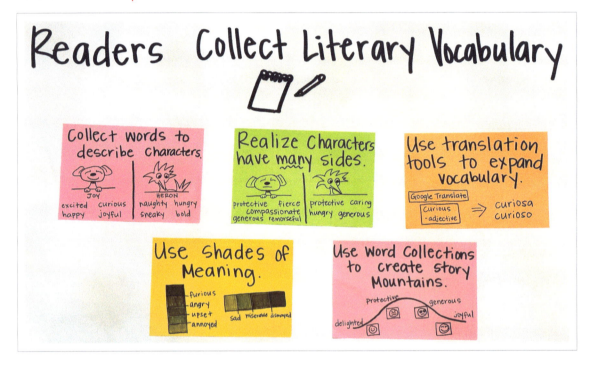

Chapter

2

Deepening Literary Vocabulary Through Writing and Talking About Reading

The Scope of These Lessons— What's Going to Happen!

The writing about reading lessons in this chapter deepen learners' engagement with literary vocabulary and encourage contextual application. They especially encourage your young linguists to write and talk about what they are reading with sophisticated, nuanced vocabulary, and therefore sophisticated, nuanced interpretation. Each lesson introduces a new strategy for sketchnoting as a way to highlight literary vocabulary, leading readers to think and talk at a highly inferential level, with a lot of text detail, about characters in the stories. These lessons build on the learning of those in Chapter 1, so I suggest that you teach those lessons on collecting literary vocabulary before these, which focus on incorporating literary vocabulary into writing about reading and literary conversations.

Lessons that teach children thoughtful strategies for writing about reading are often reading lessons in disguise, and you'll find that's true here. Teaching a child how to use an emotional timeline to explore the highs and lows of a character's emotions is really a reading lesson in character volatility. Teaching children to map the pressures characters experience is really a reading lesson on character motivation. There is a lot of very strong research demonstrating that writing about reading plays a highly important role in reading comprehension. One of the most important studies is the Carnegie Corporation report published by the Alliance for Excellent Education (2010), called *Writing to Read: Evidence for How Writing Can Improve Reading*, which found that writing about reading improves students' retention and comprehension. The question for teachers, then, is how to get children to fall in love with writing about reading, and the answer usually isn't workbooks, book reports, or reading logs (useful though those may occasionally be).

Writing to Read, Alliance for Excellent Education

For me, and for many teachers I've learned with, the answer to how to get children to fall in love with writing about reading has been sketchnoting. What's lovely about sketchnoting is that so many kinds of readers are very drawn to it, including multilingual learners, neurodiverse learners, and avid readers (Ajayi, 2008; Alhassan and Osei, 2022). Even readers who don't love to pause and jot (often avid readers fall into this category) are intrigued by sketchnoting. It's fast, it's creative, and it leads to layered literary conversations.

Sketchnoting is a little different from other kinds of writing about reading. It departs from workbooks, graphic organizers, and filling in small boxes as reading responses, in favor of children keeping a notebook, digital or analog, where they respond to texts in creative and authentic ways. If your curriculum has children in some kind of workbook for reading response (increasingly true for many large-scale reading curricula), then you can incorporate these lessons as a way to increase student creativity and agency. If for some reason reading notebooks feels like too much to add in, then children can keep this work with their vocabulary collections, perhaps in a nice presentation envelope.

There are some great texts on sketchnoting if you'd like to read more. You might enjoy the article by Katrina Schwartz on how a teacher incorporated sketchnoting as a method for improving engagement with texts, including complex texts: "Why Teachers Are So Excited About the Power of Sketchnoting" (2019). I also like Paige Tutt's post for Edutopia, "How—and Why—to Introduce Visual Note-Taking to Your Students" (2021). Paige shares research that demonstrates that more students remember more of what they learn when they sketch than when they write. Something about the process stimulates students to think about what they are learning. I'd also consider following Nichole Carter (@nichole444) who has done a tremendous amount of work in sketchnoting. She has a beautiful book, *Sketchnoting in the Classroom* (2019), and lots of online resources as well.

There is also a lot of research that supports incorporating drawing in language acquisition for multilingual learners. As in the lessons in Chapter 1, you'll once again encourage your multilingual learners to translanguage and translate as they apply and extend their literary vocabulary. In 2022, the *International Journal on Social and Educational Sciences* published an article called "Effectiveness of Integrating Drawing in Teaching English Language in Intellectual Disability Classroom" (Alhassan and Osei, 2022). This is only one among many research studies that suggest that drawing helps with language acquisition. I like this particular article for how it suggests that drawing supports students with learning differences as well as multilingual learners. In Patricia Martínez-Álvarez's book, *Teaching Emergent Bilingual Students with Dis/Abilities: Humanizing Pedagogies to Engage Learners and Eliminate Labels* (2023), we find a similar plea for pedagogy that embraces students' linguistic assets, and allows them to express their learning in multiple ways. Incorporating sketchnoting as valid reading response helps to create more pathways for children to develop and demonstrate their thinking.

As well as sketchnoting, and talking from their sketches, the final lesson of the chapter engages students in "talking in essay." In this lesson, you'll teach learners to talk in full paragraphs, with structure and academic transitions. This is incredible preparation for literary essays, and it also is just good coaching for literary conversation. Children usually respond very quickly, and the work combines literary and academic vocabulary in fluid, contextual discussions.

Almost all the lessons in this chapter are demonstrated with writing about a gorgeous picture book: *Evelyn del Rey Is Moving Away*, written by Meg Medina and illustrated by Sonia Sánchez (2020). It's a story of a young girl, Daniela, whose best friend, Evelyn del Rey, is moving far away. They have a single last day together, and choose to spend it playing their favorite, imaginative games. It's a story about love and loss and loneliness and grief. It's about how little power children often have. It's about the sustaining force of friendship and the devastation wreaked when it is ripped away. And it's a story about hope and maturity. Like so many of the new generation of picture books written by YA authors, it suggests and rewards complex interpretation work.

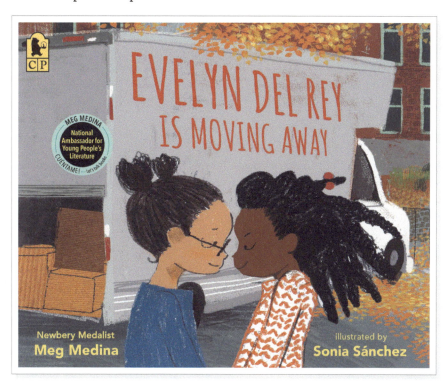

You can read *Evelyn del Rey Is Moving Away* easily in one sitting. In Lesson 1, you'll mirror the work you did in Lesson 1 of Chapter 1, collecting words to describe Daniela, and you'll add in sorting children's word collections into language palettes. Linguist Elfrieda Hiebert describes how whereas in nonfiction, authors tend to repeat expert vocabulary often, fiction writers don't. Instead, they will vary words for the same thing, so that a fire sometimes **glimmers**, it sometimes **shimmers**, it sometimes **flickers** (Hiebert, 2020). In the same way, a character is not always described as **brave**, but may also be described as **stubborn**, **courageous**, **faithful**, **determined**. You'll invite learners first to collect vocabulary to describe Daniela, the main character, and then to think about the kind of palette that Meg Medina generates around Daniela.

Two of the lessons in this chapter return to *Joy and Heron*—these lessons explore character collisions and point of view. The first investigates how characters affect each other—how, when they collide, a character can be changed. The second lesson explores moments when characters see and feel things very differently. For the work at hand in both of these lessons, Evelyn and Daniela are just too similar to nudge students to the kind of complex thinking about characters changing each other that is required. Evelyn is a mirror for Daniela in *Evelyn del Rey Is Moving Away*, whereas in most stories, the main character is changed by, or changes, other, dissimilar characters. If you want to introduce a new narrative for these lessons, rather than returning to *Joy and Heron*, I also love the digital narrative, *Supporting Act*, where the father and daughter see things very differently, and affect each other dramatically, or the picture book, *Last Stop on Market Street*, by Matt de la Peña, in which CJ and Nana experience things so differently.

Learning Goals

Expect your learners to deepen their literary vocabulary as they both learn new words and apply increasingly familiar literary vocabulary to new characters. Expect their literary conversations to be text-based and detailed and highly inferential. Expect children to enjoy writing about reading—some of them for the first time. Expect them to surprise you with their creativity and perspicacity.

Here are some specific learning goals that are built into this work:

- To deepen and extend learner's literary vocabulary.

- To raise the level of students' literary conversations—highlighting nuanced vocabulary and nuanced ideas.

- To learn a toolkit of high-leverage strategies for writing about reading that lead to thoughtful interpretation.

- To increase usage through sketchnoting and talking about stories, with an emphasis on incorporating literary vocabulary.

- To increase students' fluency with "talking in essay"—rehearsing their ideas and evidence in preparation for literary conversation or literary essay.

Text Recommendations

I suggest launching this work with a picture book so that students can continue to find details in the illustrations that support their ideas about characters. Since YA authors like Matt de la Peña and Jaqueline Woodson started writing picture books, the landscape of these books has become one of ever deepening complexity and diversity. These illustrated books are beautiful and significant. They take up social issues, they deepen representation, they suggest complicated interpretation. I love to include them as read-aloud texts, and as book club texts. Here, I demonstrate these lessons with *Evelyn del Rey Is Moving Away*. I love the emotional depth of the story, the devastating sense of impending loss that haunts the narrative. I love the beauty of the language and the grace of the translanguaging. I love the secrets about friendship and community that are hidden in the illustrations. There are many important, gorgeous picture books, of course, and I encourage you to think about the linguistic and cultural histories in your classroom community, as you make your own personal choice—the lessons in this chapter are easily transferable. Here are some favorites you might try as you return to these concepts for extra practice.

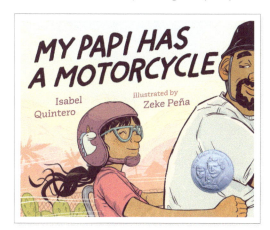

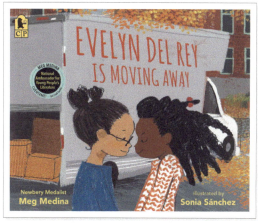

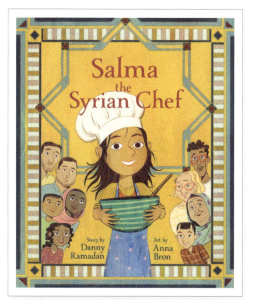

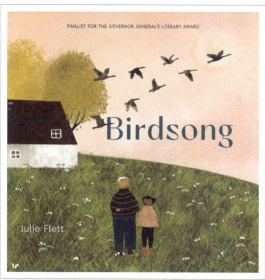

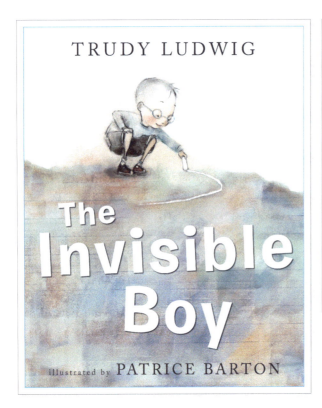

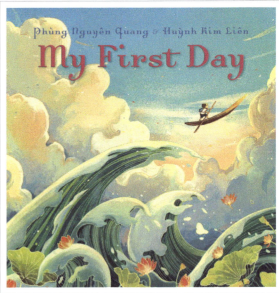

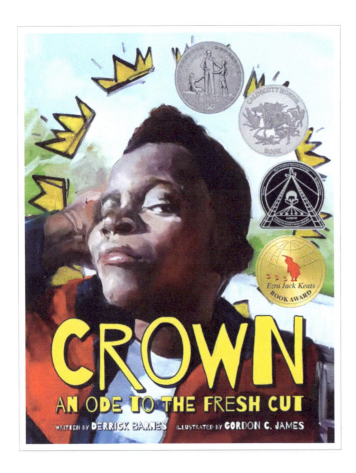

- *My Papi Has a Motorcycle*, written by Isabel Quintero, illustrated by Zeke Peña

- *Evelyn del Rey Is Moving Away*, written by Meg Medina, illustrated by Sonia Sánchez

- *Salma the Syrian Chef*, written by Danny Ramadan, illustrated by Anna Bron

- *Watercress*, written by Andrea Wang, illustrated by Jason Chin

- *Last Stop on Market Street*, by Matt de la Peña, illustrated by Christian Robinson

- *Birdsong*, written and illustrated by Julie Flett

- *The Invisible Boy*, written by Trudy Ludwig, illustrated by Patrice Barton

- *My First Day*, written and illustrated by Phùng Nguyên Quang and Huynh Kim Liên

- *Crown*, written by Derrick Barnes, illustrated by Gordon C. James

- *I Talk Like a River*, written by Jordan Scott, illustrated by Sydney Smith

Opportunities for Transfer and Application

Your learners will think deeply about literary vocabulary, increase their usage, and extend their word collections in the lessons. They'll become more fluent and creative with their writing about reading as well. All of that learning will happen inside of the 12–15 minutes of each of these lessons, as students engage in thinking, jotting, and talking. But learners will get even more out of this work if you create opportunities for them to apply these writing and talking about reading strategies to fresh texts. You might create an anchor chart to document the strategies you've taught, as a reminder for students, and then incorporate these strategies into your reading curriculum, adding to children's options for reading response.

An anchor chart helps learners remember and transfer skills and habits

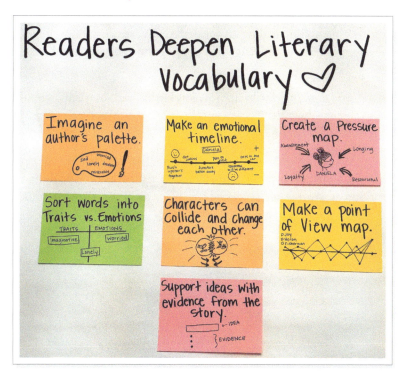

For instance, you might fold this work into ways that book clubs respond to their texts and prepare for book club conversations. You might add a micro unit on reading response—reading notebooks and writing about reading—to your curriculum. Every time that readers have the opportunity to think more deeply about what they are reading, to sketch and jot in ways that help them to develop new ideas and share those with others, and to reach for precise, literary vocabulary, they become more proficient readers, writers, and thinkers. Deepening literary vocabulary through sketchnoting and talking about reading fits beautifully with:

- character studies

- book clubs

- literary essays

- reading response curriculum

- intervention groups

- enrichment groups

Assessment Options

You should see an increase in the depth and nuance of students' literary conversation, and in the specificity and creativity of their writing about reading. As was true for the work of Chapter 1, measuring vocabulary knowledge is tricky, as it is unconstrained. But you can pay attention to its application—how students use it in context. Some possibilities for assessment (including self-assessment) include:

- *Reading response.* Collect students' writing about reading responses, assessing them for ideas about characters, text evidence, literary vocabulary, and explanation.

- *Preparation for book club, and book club conversations.* Listen to or record club conversations, noting how groups use their writing about reading to generate conversation, how they incorporate literary vocabulary, how they support their thinking with detail from the text, and how they build on each other's thinking.

- *Literary essay, rehearsal, and drafting.* Evaluate how students "'talk in essay," about their ideas about characters. Note how they use specific literary vocabulary to express their ideas, how they use academic transitions to move from one example or part of their idea to the next, how they support their ideas with details from the text, and how they incorporate a brief intro and conclusion.

- *Students' word collections.* Note the appropriateness of words learners have linked to specific characters, and the kinds of words they have collected (for example, Tier 2 words, cognates, translating across languages), as they extend their word collections.

Links to Standards

Reading Anchor Standard 1: Read closely to determine what the text says explicitly/implicitly and make logical inferences from it; cite specific textual evidence when writing or speaking to support conclusions drawn from the text.

Reading Anchor Standard 2: Determine central ideas or themes of a text and analyze their development; summarize the key supporting details and ideas.

Reading Anchor Standard 3: Analyze how and why individuals, events, and ideas develop and interact over the course of a text.

Reading Anchor Standard 4: Interpret words and phrases as they are used in a text, including determining technical, connotative, and figurative meanings, and analyze how specific word choices shape meaning or tone.

Reading Anchor Standard 5: Analyze the structure of texts.

Reading Anchor Standard 6: Assess how point of view or purpose shapes the content and style of a text, drawing on a wide range of global and diverse texts.

Reading Anchor Standard 7: Integrate and evaluate content presented in diverse media and formats.

Language Anchor Standard 5: Demonstrate understanding of figurative language, word relationships, and nuances in word meanings.

Language Anchor Standard 6: Acquire and accurately use general academic and content-specific words and phrases sufficient for reading, writing, speaking, and listening; demonstrate independence in gathering and applying vocabulary knowledge when considering a word or phrase important to comprehension or expression.

Lesson 2.1

Authors' Palettes

Considerations

Lesson summary: In this session you will read-aloud *Evelyn del Rey Is Moving Away*, written by Meg Medina and illustrated by Sonia Sánchez, and you will launch students into sketchnoting as a form of writing about reading and deepening literary vocabulary. You'll begin by inviting learners to collect words to describe the narrator, Daniela, as they did for Joy and Heron. Then you'll show learners how to imagine an author's palette, and to think about what shades of characteristics readers perceive Daniela washed with. Students will sketch palettes and sort words into these (such as the many words for **sad**), and then explain their decisions to a partner.

This work gives your learners an opportunity to repeat the strategy of collecting words to describe characters, thus increasing students' independence and their usage of literary vocabulary. As children consider the palette Daniela is washed with, they also have another opportunity to sort words into semantic groups. In their literary conversations they develop new insights about how many characters have a dominant shade (**merry**, **melancholic**, **angry**).

Estimated lesson time: 15–20 minutes.

Materials and preparation: You'll need a copy of the picture book. You and your students will need a place to sketch and collect words—such as a reader's notebook—that learners can use across these lessons, or simply paper and a place for children to keep their word collections and sketchnotes. Visit the website www.vocabularyconnections.org to download a printable blank palette.

In the launch of the lesson, you'll also display two paintings to demonstrate lighter and darker palettes. For example, I use two from the Art Institute of Chicago.

Sandwich with Soda, Roy Lichtenstein, Art Institute of Chicago

Greyed Rainbow, Jackson Pollock, Art Institute of Chicago

Additional lesson options: This lesson suggests a palette as a metaphor for how readers perceive characters. Elfrieda Hiebert, in *Teaching Words and How They Work* (2020), examines the palette as the kinds of word groups fiction authors literally use to describe things that reoccur in a particular story. For instance, if there are a lot of fires in a story, instead of writing repeatedly that the fire **glimmers**, the author might write **gleam** or **flicker** or **glisten** or **twinkle**. If your students are reading longer chapter books, they can investigate these semantic clusters of words that appear again and again. Some characters, for instance, are described with many words for **lonely** or **impulsive** or **brave**. Some places are described with a variety of words as well such as **claustrophobic** or **frightening**.

Launching the Lesson

Remind students of the work they did with *Joy and Heron* collecting literary vocabulary to describe the characters. Introduce Daniela, the main character of *Evelyn del Rey Is Moving Away*, and invite learners to do similar work, collecting words to describe Daniela. Set up your sticky notes, and have learners do the same. Also alert students to the upcoming work of all these lessons, which will be sketchnoting to develop new thinking and to deepen their vocabulary.

The start of today's work should feel familiar to students. You might say, "Readers, linguists, we're going to read a new story today. It's called *Evelyn del Rey Is Moving Away*. The author is Meg Medina, and the illustrator is Sonia Sánchez. The story is told by the main character, the narrator Daniela. We'll start by collecting words to describe Daniela, so take a moment to set up your notes, and I'll do the same."

To rally students for the work to come, you might say, "Readers, across the next few days, you'll be diving into writing about reading—but you'll be focusing especially on sketchnoting. Today you'll make a bit of a start with this—in a bit, you'll be doing some sketching and then sorting the words you gather around a sketch, which is why sticky notes will be helpful, so you can move your words around."

Engagement—Collecting Words, Sketchnoting, and Oral Language Practice

Read aloud, pausing to jot words, and to invite students to do the same. Offer direct instruction, teaching new words.

You might start by saying, "As I read the story, you know what to do. Start jotting words to describe Daniela."

After a few pages, stop to give readers a moment to share their words. You might say, "Let's compare your words, readers, with a partner. Talk to them about the words you came up with to describe Daniela and the details in the story that support your thinking."

Then you might teach new words, saying, "Readers, as we think about how terribly sad Daniela is at losing Evelyn, I want to teach you a new word using a word equation. When someone is **sad** and also **hopeless**, like they don't think they can change things, then the word for that feeling is **disconsolate**. It feels like Daniela is **disconsolate**, as Evelyn gets into the car to leave forever."

You might also offer direct instruction that will build toward the palette work you'll introduce in a moment by teaching a new word collection. You might say, "I want to teach you a few new words. They describe Daniela and Evelyn and how **creative** they are. I'm not thinking about a vertical, but more a word collection. For instance, other words for **creative** include **imaginative**—that's when you're good at using your imagination—or **inventive**—that's when you can invent new things, both real and imaginary—and **resourceful**—that's when you can use what's at hand to make things."

Invite partners to discuss the words and their relation to the characters. "Talk to your partner. When are Daniela and Evelyn **imaginative, inventive, resourceful**? What evidence in the story is there? What other words might go in this collection? What other words seem important in describing Daniela? … oh, yes, I love that word, **innovative**, which also means **inventive**."

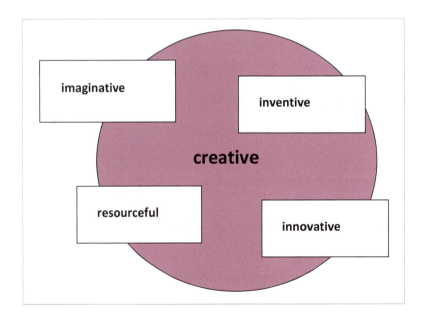

Introduce the notion of palettes. Then give students time to sketch palettes and sort some of their words into these, and to discuss with a partner.

You can build directly on the word collection for **creative**, to introduce palettes. You might say, "Linguists, I want to teach you something new about how you might group words. When artists paint, they use what's called a palette, and they'll put a few colors on that palette" (Sketch a palette). "Some artists use a palette of mostly very bright colors—like Roy Lichtenstein in this painting. Others use a palette of very dark colors, like Jackson Pollock in this painting."

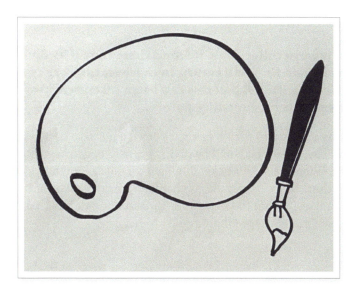

As you continue your introduction to authors' palettes, you might say, "We can think about authors as having palettes they use to paint characters too. Watch this. I've sketched this palette. Now I'm going to think about how it feels like Daniela is painted in certain shades. I'm thinking, for instance, that Daniela is painted in shades of **sadness** and **worry** across this story. So we can move all our words that fit that palette onto this palette. I'll do that, and you do it as well."

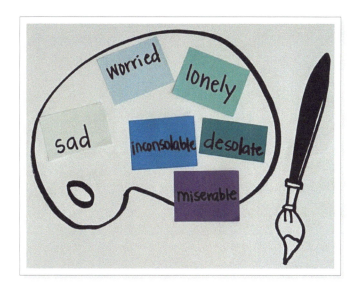

You can also coach children in how some characters are painted with more than one shade. You might say, "Readers, it's true that Daniela is **sad** and **worried** throughout most of this story. But it also feels like there is a second palette for Daniela. Do you agree that we could also say that Daniela is also painted with shades of **creativity**, and maybe also of **love**? Take a minute, and sketch another palette, and move words to it, if you think Daniela is painted by more than one palette. Then share with your partner."

Application

Make sure children keep their word collections. Remind them they'll be diving more deeply into sketchnoting, and they will return to these words as they do so. Also suggest that thinking about authors' palettes can be an interesting way to pay attention to language whenever they are reading a story.

To encourage children to use this strategy to sort vocabulary words, but also to pay attention to authors' language, you might say, "Readers, you'll be diving more deeply into sketchnoting over the next few days. Today you made a start at sketching with a quick sketch of a palette, that you used to sort words, to think more deeply about characters. You can do this work with any story you are reading. You can also begin to notice and think about palettes that authors use, what word collections you see in the chapter books you are reading."

The work students will create during and after the lesson might look like ...

Book club members collect a palette of words to reflect Daniela's sadness

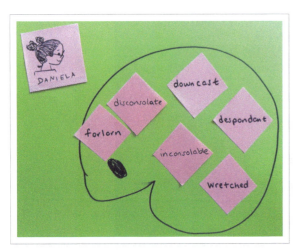

Returning to word equations

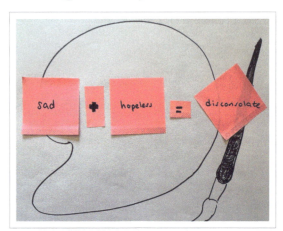

Winn Dixie's palette in *Because of Winn Dixie*

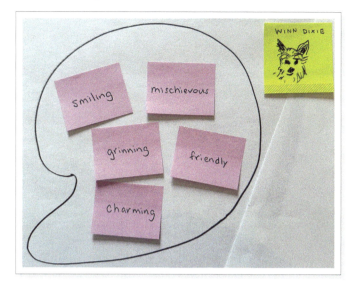

Emotional Timelines

Considerations

Lesson summary: In this session you will teach students a sketchnoting strategy—sketching an emotional timeline, a kind of electrocardiogram (EKG) of a character's emotions. You'll practice with Daniela, the narrator of *Evelyn del Rey Is Moving Away*. You'll sketch and label a timeline, and students will make their own as well, and then explain their choices to their partner. You'll demonstrate choosing specific, literary vocabulary to describe Daniela's emotions, and you'll encourage children to do the same while using their verticals to help them choose words. You'll also teach some new words to describe Daniela's traits and emotions.

This work deepens students' engagement with literary vocabulary and gives them an opportunity for highly contextual application and literary conversations.

Estimated lesson time: 15 minutes.

Materials and preparation: You'll need the picture book, and you'll sketch an emotional timeline as a demonstration. Learners will need their notebook or paper where they can sketch their own versions of an emotional timeline. You and your students will need copies of verticals from lesson 1.4. Visit the website, www.vocabularyconnections.org, to download sample verticals.

Additional lesson options: Sometimes children suggest spin-offs of this work, setting a different axis on their timeline. They'll trace power, for instance, tracing the times and ways a character feels **powerful** or **powerless**, or they'll trace **hopeful** and **hopeless**, or **faithful** and **disloyal**. If you have students in book clubs, you might pull a club together, and invite them to think about the different contrasting states their characters experience.

Launching the Lesson

Suggest students have their word collections and palettes for Daniela to hand. Compliment learners on how their literary vocabulary is growing, and how collecting words has deepened their literary conversations. Then talk about writing about reading and sketchnoting as important ways to deepen their engagement with stories.

It's helpful to create cohesion across the work students take up on different days. Here, you might begin by saying, "Linguists, I want to compliment you on how your literary vocabulary is growing. I hear you using more sophisticated words to describe characters. I see how your collections of literary vocabulary are leading you to speak with more depth and precision about characters and stories."

It's also helpful to stir up interest in new work, so students know why they are doing it. You might say, for example, "Today I want to share some research with you. It's from a famous educational study called 'Write to Read'. Think about the title, what it suggests ... yes, this study showed that kids who write about their reading read better! They have more to say about what they're reading, and they remember what they read more."

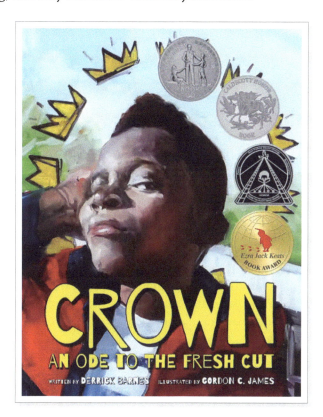

Then you can give a little tip, as a way to introduce sketchnoting. "But the question you might be asking is: what kind of writing about reading makes the most difference? And I'll give you a tip, also from research. It turns out that sketchnoting—adding in sketches to your writing about reading—deepens learners' thinking! So that's what we'll be doing. You started a bit yesterday, with your sketches of palettes. I'm going to teach you a few different ways to sketchnote, that will give you a chance to deepen your literary vocabulary, and will also let you work creatively to develop some interesting thinking about what you're reading."

Engagement—Sketchnoting and Literary Conversations

Demonstrate how to set up an emotional timeline, and invite students to get theirs set up. Then read the beginning of the story, showing how you add to your timeline by thinking about precise words to describe the ups and downs of Daniela's emotions.

You don't need to do a deep demonstration. This is more of an implicit model to get children started. You might say, "We're going to start, today, with emotional timelines. These are a kind of EKG, like a heart monitor, of a character's emotions. Your emotional timeline will show when the character's emotions go up, in a positive direction, and when they go down, in a negative direction. Watch how I set up my page."

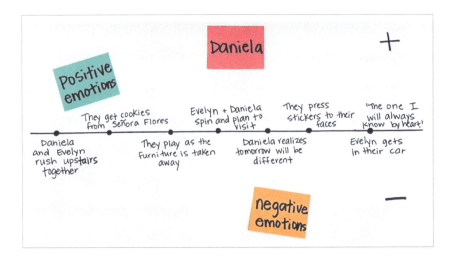

Try to keep an invitational tone so that your learners feel a sense of agency. It might sound like: "You don't have to set up your page exactly like mine, though it helps to have enough room to track the ups and downs of a character's emotions. And our main character's name is Daniela, so you might want to label your timeline somewhere with her name. You can also decide if you want to use any colors on your timeline. I think I'm going to use black to label the events, or moments on the timeline, and blue for Daniela's emotions. Let's start by adding in the big moments in the story."

Show how you use a vertical to explore shades of meaning. Be sure to give partners time to share with each other, so they engage in literary conversations, using their emotional timelines as starting points for these text-based conversations.

As you reread or skim the text, you can continue to model by pausing to add emotions to your timeline, turning to a vertical to seek precise language. It might sound like, "Hmm, I feel like at this moment, when Daniela is planning for how far away Evelyn will be, I want to look at the vertical for **sad**. It feels like Daniela is all different kinds of **sad**, and that as we get near the end of the story, she is really **sad**, like maybe **miserable**. Maybe even **inconsolable**, which is really, really **sad**, so **sad** nothing can make you feel better. Use your verticals too, and choose very precise words to describe Daniela's emotions. I'm thinking that the vertical for happy will also be important, because there are moments when Daniela is very happy as they play. Do a little sketching and jotting. Then share with your partner. Why did you choose those precise words?"

Evelyn Del Rey is moving away.
So she won't be right here anymore.

Application

Have children keep their emotional timelines at the start of a sketchnoting collection. You might suggest a gallery walk in a few days, for learners to share some of their sketchnotes—this increases engagement. Suggest, as well, that children can use this strategy to analyze any volatile character.

It's lovely to affirm student learning. You might say, "I want to compliment you on the way you used your verticals to explore shades of meaning. I saw some of you adding new words to your verticals. And I definitely heard you talking about Daniela's emotions with very precise, literary vocabulary. Well done."

If you expect to share readers' writing about reading pages in a gallery walk, you might suggest: "Readers, when you are sketchnoting, it's often helpful, after you finish, to look over what you've created, and then jot a sticky note, or add a box, where you sum up your thinking—essentially you ask yourself, 'What is this making me think?' Then when another reader studies your page, they'll be able to follow your thinking."

If you are sending children off to transfer this work to another reading experience, it might sound like: "Readers, that was beautiful work you did with Daniela. And of course sketching and labeling an emotional timeline will help you investigate any character's emotions. A lot of characters in the stories you are reading are **volatile**—that means very **changeable**. As you are reading, then, and preparing for book club or class discussions, you can begin an emotional timeline as a way to investigate a character's emotions, their **volatility**."

The work students will create during and after the lesson might look like ...

An emotional timeline for Daniela

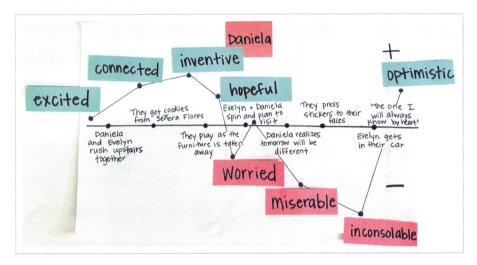

Tracing Daisy's emotions in *My Papi Has a Motorcycle*

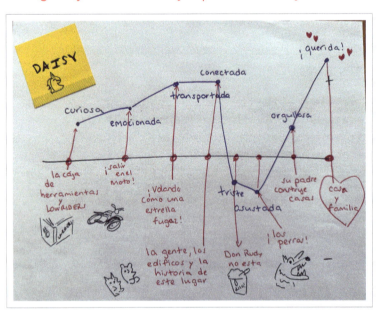

Lesson 2.3

Pressure Maps

Considerations

Lesson summary: In this session you will teach students another writing about reading strategy—sketching a pressure map. In a pressure map, the reader labels the variety of pressures on a character, striving for precise, literary vocabulary to describe these pressures. Children usually pick this strategy up easily as soon as you demonstrate—they have a lot of pressures in their own lives. In this case, for Daniela, she feels the pressure of **loneliness, abandonment** by a friend, **longing** to have things never change, the urge to stay **connected**. You'll sketch and label a pressure map, and students will make their own as well, and then explain their choices to their partner. You'll demonstrate choosing specific, literary vocabulary to describe Daniela's pressures, and you'll encourage children to do the same, and to use their verticals to help them choose words. You'll also teach some new words to describe some of the pressures Daniela experiences.

This work both deepens and extends children's literary vocabulary, and often learners come to new insights about character motivation—why characters feel and act the way they do. It also creates new opportunities for rich, text-based literary conversation.

Estimated lesson time: 12 minutes.

Materials and preparation: You'll need the picture book to remind readers of specific moments. You'll need paper and markers. Students will need their reading notebooks and markers, or paper and markers, as well.

Additional lesson options: As students become more proficient with sketchnoting, it's helpful to set up opportunities for them to share with an audience. Gallery walks are a great way for students to share and to inspire each other. Invite learners to have a favorite page ready for Friday, for instance. Letting readers know they'll be sharing often inspires them to work with care and attention to detail. Pressure mapping is also a great collecting strategy for narrative writing. Young people feel tremendous pressures, in so many ways.

Launching the Lesson

Remind students of the emotional timelines they created, and compliment them on paying attention to detail in the story, on inferring the main character's emotions, and on reaching for literary vocabulary. Then introduce the new sketchnoting strategy, pressure maps.

It always helps to review the work students did recently and connect it to today's work. You might say, "Readers, linguists, you did some thoughtful work yesterday when you created emotional timelines for Daniela. You really paid attention to details in the story, including details in the illustrations, to support your ideas, and you also reached for precise, literary vocabulary."

To introduce today's work, you might say, "Today I'm sharing another sketchnoting strategy with you, one that really gets readers thinking deeply about what shapes a character—what they experience that causes them to feel and act the way they do. It's a pressure map."

Engagement—Sketchnoting and Literary Conversations

Demonstrate how you set up a pressure map, and how you might begin to add to it. Then invite readers to work on their own. You can coach students by teaching new words to match the pressures they describe.

Usually children simply need to see a brief model of how to get started, to know how they might set up their page. You might say, "Watch me set up a pressure map, so it's ready for me to add to it. I put the character in the center. Sometimes I sketch the character as a little figure; other times I just put their name. Then I ask myself: 'What pressures does this character face? What causes them to act and feel the way they do?'"

It is helpful to demonstrate how you think about and name pressures in a way that encourages learners to reach for literary vocabulary. You might say, "I'm thinking about how Daniela doesn't want anything to change. But she faces the terrible pressure of **abandonment**, because Evelyn is moving away. I'll add that to my map. Do you see how I reached for a precise word or phrase, to describe the pressure?"

Often, children can describe a pressure by giving examples from the story, but they don't have literary vocabulary to be precise. They might say, for example, "Daniela cries when Evelyn gets in the car." You can act as a proficient partner, saying, "Oh yes, that is a moment of terrible pressure. Do you think it might be **loneliness**, is that a pressure Daniela experiences here?"

Or if a reader talks about how Daniela seems worried about fitting everything in on this one day, you might say, "Yes, she does seem **rushed** and **worried**. Maybe that's the pressure of **foreshadowing of loss**! She knows what is going to happen at the end of the day."

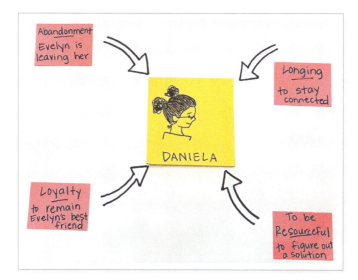

You can also encourage students to use phrases, such as **wanting to stay connected** or **terrified of losing her best friend**.

Once children have worked on their own pressure maps, invite them to share with their partner. Encourage them to explain their thinking, using details from the story and the illustrations to support their ideas.

This kind of sketchnoting leads to deep conversations about characters' experiences and motivations. You might say, "I can tell you are going to have a lot to say. Use your pressure maps to explain to each other some of the pressures Daniela experiences. How do these pressures influence her feelings and her actions?"

Remind multilingual learners to label in all their languages, and use their translation tools as well.

You might say, "Sometimes there is a phrase or word that you know better in your first language. Jot that down! You can use translation tools with your partner to figure out the precise words in English."

Application

Have children keep their pressure maps as part of their collection of sketchnotes. Remind them they can use this sketchnoting strategy to think deeply about characters whenever they are reading.

You might say, "Readers, you did some deep thinking about Daniela. I'll teach you a new word. When a reader is **thoughtful**, and really pays attention to details in a story to come up with ideas, we say that the reader is **insightful**. You've been **insightful** today! Keep your pressure maps. Whenever you are reading and talking about stories, sketching pressure maps will help you be more **insightful** about characters' motivations—why they feel and act the way they do."

If you are also teaching narrative writing, you might say, "Pressure maps can also be a great strategy when you are writing stories. They help you think about what shapes a character, and how you can show that in your writing."

The work students will create during and after the lesson might look like ...

The pressures on Heron shape his traits and emotions

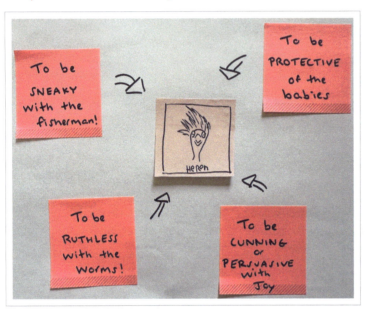

Pip faces many pressures as he strives to become a guide dog

Traits vs. Emotions T-Charts

Considerations

Lesson summary: In this session you will teach students a new writing about reading strategy that supports weighing and evaluating whether a characteristic is a trait or an emotion. Using their word collections for Daniela, partners will move a few of these words onto a T-Chart of Traits/Emotions, and explain why they think a word describes a trait versus an emotion. For instance, it's interesting to ask: Does Daniela seem like a **worried** and **inconsolable** child overall, or does she seem **inconsolable** right now because she is losing a friend?

This work gives learners an opportunity to ponder characters' emotional states and inner qualities, to think about the difference between traits and emotions, and to use their literary vocabulary in text-based discussion.

Estimated lesson time: 12 minutes.

Materials and preparation: You'll need a collection of words to describe Daniela, from your initial read-aloud. You'll also create a simple T-Chart to sort traits vs. emotions. Students will create their own word T-Charts as well. It's helpful for them to have verticals on hand also.

Additional lesson options: If your classroom community includes students whose first language is Spanish, or who are learning Spanish, this lesson translates in interesting ways into a study of *ser* vs. *estar*. Several teachers have found this lesson to be very helpful to think about character traits as *ser* and emotional states as *estar*, as a way to both deepen students' understanding of characters and of this language system.

Launching the Lesson

Sum up the sketchnoting students have done so far (palettes, emotional timelines, pressure maps), and give them a moment to review these and all the words they've used to describe Daniela. Then let learners know they'll need their word collection for Daniela, and invite them to have these on hand either as a collection of sticky notes or notes on palettes. Suggest, as well, that they should have their verticals on hand.

You might say, "Readers, take a moment to review with your partner the sketchnoting you've done so far. Show your partner your palettes, emotional timelines, and pressure maps. Explain what you've learned about Daniela, what insights you have about her, and what words precisely describe her."

To organize your learners for the upcoming lesson you might say, "Readers, today you're going to try a new sketchnoting strategy. You'll need three things. You'll need to sketch a T-Chart and label the two columns **Traits** and **Emotions**. You'll need your word collection for Daniela. That means the sticky notes you wrote and your palettes, if a lot of your words are on palettes. And finally, you should have your verticals at hand."

Engagement—Collecting Words and Oral Language Practice

Demonstrate how to take a word from your collection, and ponder whether it is more of a trait or an emotion, giving an explanation of each.

You might say, "Watch me try this—and be ready to say if you agree with my thinking. I'm thinking about how Daniela seems so **worried**. She's **worried** a lot, actually, across the story, about losing Evelyn. But I feel like she's not a girl who normally worries. The way Daniela describes her friendship with Evelyn, it feels like a very solid friendship. So I'm going to put **worried** as an emotion—Daniela is **worried** in response to something that's happening right now in her life."

Then you might engage partners in weighing and evaluating another word with you. "Now you try. What about **imaginative**? Does that seem like a fleeting state, something temporary, for Daniela? Or do you think being **imaginative** is a way Daniela often is, something inside her, so it's a trait? Talk to your partner."

Invite readers to ponder a word that it's less clear if it is a trait or an emotion or might be in flux. Then encourage them to keep going with this work, with their partner.

You might say, "Readers, as you try out this work, know that sometimes a word might be hard to figure out—maybe it's unclear if it is a trait and an emotion, or it starts as one thing and becomes another. For instance, I'm wondering about **lonely**. Daniela hasn't been **lonely**, but now that Evelyn is leaving, might she become sort of permanently **lonely**? Might it become a trait? You can talk about that with your partner as you keep going with this work."

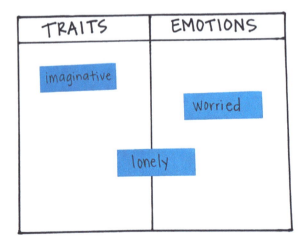

Application

Recap the work students did, of focusing on literary vocabulary to be precise in their language, and of weighing and evaluating whether a word describes a trait or an emotion. Suggest that this strategy will lead to insights whenever they are analyzing characters.

You might say, "Readers, this work, of weighing and evaluating traits versus emotions, often leads to new insights about characters. Whenever you are analyzing characters in stories, know that you can jot a quick T-Chart, and then ponder words that go in either column, or might be in the middle, because they indicate a character is changing."

The work students will create during and after the lesson might look like ...

Ser vs. estar en *Joy y Heron*

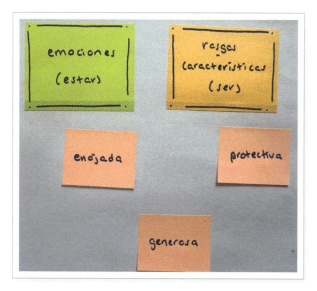

Tracing Katniss's emotions and traits in *The Hunger Games*

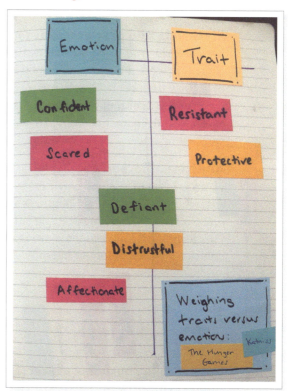

Character Collisions

Considerations

Lesson summary: In this session you'll show students how in many stories, when characters collide, one character changes another. You'll return to *Joy and Heron* to explore this notion, and you'll demonstrate how to sketchnote to capture these collisions and their impact. This work gives learners more oral practice with literary vocabulary, it helps them apply these words contextually, and it deepens their insight into character change and cause and effect.

Estimated lesson time: 12 minutes.

Materials and preparation: You'll need your original word collection for *Joy and Heron*, and you'll show the video again. You'll also sketchnote a visual of Joy and Heron as if they were asteroids colliding, with room to jot or move words below the sketch (or you can download a sketch from the website www.vocabularyconnections.org). You might show an image of an asteroid and a planet colliding to launch this lesson. Here is an example of a compelling one.

Additional lesson options: If you don't want to return to *Joy and Heron*, and instead want to introduce a new narrative for this lesson, I love the digital narrative, *Supporting Act*, where the father and daughter affect each other dramatically, or the picture book, *Last Stop on Market Street*, by Matt de la Peña, in which Nana's acceptance of people changes CJ's feelings. If your students are reading longer chapter books, they'll see more character collisions as well in longer narratives.

Launching the Lesson

Introduce the notion of characters colliding with a metaphor of asteroids and planets colliding, and explain that often, in collisions, characters change each other.

You might say, "Readers, I want to start today by showing you a couple of images of objects colliding in space. Astronomers see asteroids and planets and gas giants colliding in the solar system. When they collide, change happens. Sometimes an asteroid is shattered or sometimes an asteroid profoundly changes a planet."

Asteroid/planet collision

"Well, the same thing can be true when characters collide. They can change each other. Sometimes for the worse, like a character might hurt another character. Or sometimes for the better, like when one character teaches another valuable lessons."

Let students know that they'll be practicing this work with *Joy and Heron*, and demonstrate setting up your sketchnoting page.

To demonstrate setting up your page, you might say, "You'll have some good ideas for how you might sketchnote this. We're going to practice with Joy and Heron, so you'll want to make some kind of sketch that captures both characters and suggests they collide. Leave room to jot or move words that describe their traits and emotions underneath them—showing how one character affects another. I think mine is going to look like this."

Engagement—Sketchnoting and Literary Conversations

"Reread" the first part of *Joy and Heron*. Demonstrate how you think about character collisions with an early scene, where Heron first steals a worm. Do some sketchnoting, jotting, and thinking aloud about how in this collision, Heron changes Joy.

You might say, "Readers, let's try this work together. Let's reread this very early scene, where Joy first encounters Heron. See if you see a character collision … it looks like Joy starts out friendly. See her ears are up, and she's smiling, when she sees Heron? But then when Heron is sneaky, then Joy becomes upset. Definitely a character collision!"

Invite learners to find more character collisions across the story, and give them time to sketchnote and then explain their insights to their partner.

You might say, "Readers, let's give you a chance to keep going. Let's read on, and if you see a moment that you think is a character collision, give a thumbs up, and we'll pause so you have a moment to jot. Then we'll go on."

After readers have finished the narrative and jotted, you might say, "I can see you'll have a lot to talk about. I want to compliment you on how you are using your literary vocabulary, and how you're noticing when one character changes another. Share with your partner!"

Application

Suggest students remember and try this strategy with other stories they read. Suggest, as well, that they notice when in life and in history one person changes another. Often mentors and heroes create character collisions on a grand scale.

You might say, "Readers, you came to some new insights about Joy and Heron. Remember this strategy whenever you are analyzing characters. And you might begin to notice when, in life, you see people collide—for good and sometimes for bad. For those of you who love history, you'll see it in history, as well—sometimes one person has a dramatic effect on other people, often because that one person was **courageous** and **determined**, sometimes because that one person was **evil**. When you describe how characters affect each other, reach for precise, literary vocabulary."

The work students will create during and after the lesson might look like ...

Joy and Heron change each other

Colisiones de Joy y Heron—ambos cambian

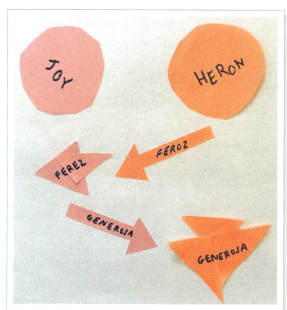

Point of View Maps

Considerations

Lesson summary: In this session you'll teach learners that often different characters experience very different emotions in a single moment, based on their point of view. You'll show students how to create point of view maps that are similar to emotional timelines (Lesson 2.2), only with more than one character's points of view traced as pathways on the timeline.

You and your students will create point of view maps, analyzing *Joy and Heron*, this time tracing the emotions of Joy, Heron, and the fisherman in a few key moments. If you want to make the lesson simpler, trace only two characters' points of view.

This work gives learners another opportunity to explore and apply their literary vocabulary contextually in literary conversations. It also develops close reading skills, especially thinking about perspective and point of view.

Estimated lesson time: 15 minutes.

Materials and preparation: You'll need your word collections for *Joy and Heron*, your verticals, paper, and three different colored markers, pens, or pencils, as well as a black one. Your students will need the same. You may decide to give some students the bare outlines of the map, with the narrative moments that you'll explore, so they don't have to take the time to jot those. Visit the website, www.vocabularyconnections.org, to download a sample.

Additional lesson options: Distinguishing different characters' points of view is tricky work for young readers (and much assessed on state ELA exams). You may decide to layer this work across more than one lesson, beginning with an emotional timeline for Joy, then adding in Heron and the fisherman in different sessions. You can also extend this work by adding in the reader's point of view. For example, when Heron and Joy fight over the worm, they feel **fierce** and **aggressive**, but I as a reader feel **amused**. A lot of young readers struggle to separate their own point of view from the characters, and this work will give them extra practice with it and a new way to visualize it.

Launching the Lesson

Remind learners of the work they did with emotional timelines. Let them know that today you'll extend that work, mapping the pathways of various characters'

points of view—how different characters feel at the same moment. Then demonstrate how to set up a point of view map for *Joy and Heron*.

You might begin, "Readers, find your emotional timelines, the ones you sketched for Daniela. Remind your partner how an emotional timeline works, how you create one. Today, we're going to extend this work. We're going to add more than one character's emotions, so that the timeline becomes more like a point of view map—it will have different paths, or emotional highways, for each character."

To set up a sketchnote page, you might say, "We're going to analyze *Joy and Heron* today to practice this work. First, we'll jot a few big moments across a timeline and set up a color key for each character. For the key, you'll need three colors, one for Joy, one for Heron, and one for the fisherman. And you'll need a black pen or marker to mark the story moments on the timeline. I'm thinking my sketch will look like this. I'll mark these big moments in the story, and you should too: the fisherman speaks sharply to Joy—Joy and Heron fight—the fisherman drives Heron off—Heron can't feed her babies—Joy gives Heron worms—Heron gives Joy and the fisherman fish."

Remind learners that this work is also about nuanced meanings of words. You might say, "You'll also want your word collections for *Joy and Heron* near you, and your verticals, so you can reach for precise, literary vocabulary, words that capture the nuances of each character's feelings."

enraged furious angry/mad upset frustrated annoyed	inconsolable desolate miserable unhappy/sad downhearted dejected	petrified terrified frightened scared timid nervous
joyful delighted happy content cheerful pleased	malevolent pitiless vicious malicious cruel/mean spiteful	compassionate empathetic kind/nice sympathetic thoughtful pleasant

Engagement—Sketchnoting and Literary Conversations

Demonstrate how you might sketchnote, using precise literary vocabulary, focusing on one moment in the story—when the fisherman first castigates Joy after she fights with Heron. Invite students to begin their maps in a similar fashion.

You might say, "Let's get started together. I'm thinking about this first moment, when Joy is caught fighting with Heron and the fisherman speaks sharply to her. I think I would say that Joy feels **chagrined** and maybe … hmm, I'm looking at words for **sad**, and I'm thinking maybe **glum**. And the fisherman's point of view is different. He feels … **mad**. Looking at the vertical for **mad**, I don't think he's **furious**, or at least not yet. I think he's more **annoyed** that Joy might be scaring off the fish. And Heron? Hmm, we don't really see her, but I'm guessing Heron may feel a little **cunning**, because she doesn't get caught!"

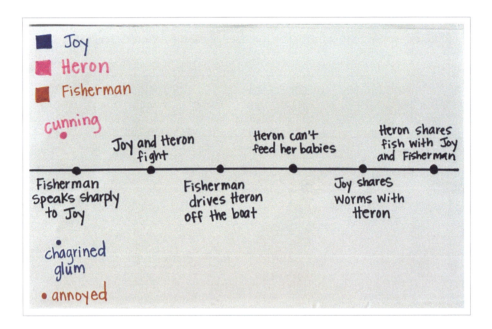

Review the steps you followed. You might say, "Do you see how I thought about each character, thinking about the precise literary vocabulary to describe each character's emotions, what they feel in that moment? I checked my key to make sure I used the right color for each character. Then I began to annotate my sketch with their emotions—and now I've started a map that captures the different points of view in this story? You start your map. What words would you use to describe each character at this moment? What colors are you using for each character? When you're ready, compare with your partner."

"Reread" *Joy and Heron*, **giving learners time to sketchnote. You may offer direct instruction, teaching new words. Then give partners time to share with each other.**

You might say, "Readers, let's go on. We'll reread *Joy and Heron*, stopping at these big moments in the story. At each moment, we'll pause so you can add to your point of view map. Remember, you can use your word collections and verticals to reach for precise literary vocabulary."

As learners work, you can coach and encourage, saying things like, "It's really powerful how you are imagining how each character might feel in that moment. It takes a sophisticated reader to distinguish between different characters' points of view."

To teach new words, you might teach the word **smug**, saying, "Readers, a lot of you are thinking about how Joy seems to feel when the fisherman drives Heron off. Look at her face! The word for that expression is **smug**. **Smug** is an interesting word. It means feeling **pleased**, or **satisfied**—but it often has a feeling of also being **justified**. Sometimes when someone is **smug**, it's often because they receive approval while someone else is being punished. That's definitely happening here!"

You can also teach the words **absorbed** and **engrossed**, saying, "I want to teach you two other new words. They are **absorbed** and **engrossed**. When someone is **absorbed** or **engrossed**, they are totally caught up in what they are doing, so they don't even notice others around them. For instance, when the fisherman doesn't notice Heron's shenanigans, it's because he is so **absorbed**, or **engrossed**, in his fishing. Tell your partner—what do you get so **absorbed**, or **engrossed** in, that you don't even notice what's happening around you? Is it reading? Music? Gaming? Use this new vocabulary. Say, 'I get really **engrossed** in …' or 'Whenever I … I'm really **absorbed** …'"

When students seem ready, give them an opportunity to share their maps, saying, "Readers, share your point of view maps with a partner. What new insights did you come to about the characters? When are their points of view similar, and when are they very different?"

Application

Suggest that learners apply this sketchnoting strategy to other reading experiences, as a way to investigate point of view. Also encourage them to think about how others, in any moment in our lives, might experience different emotions from ours, and we can try to describe our own emotions with nuanced language while, at the same time, understanding how others are feeling.

You might say, "Readers, you can apply this strategy whenever you are analyzing characters in a story. Often characters feel very different things at the same moment—they have different points of view. This can be true in life as well. Sometimes people don't understand each other's feelings. Learning to describe your own feelings with precise language, and to understand others' feelings, is part of becoming a more empathetic person, as well as a more powerful reader."

The work students will create during and after the lesson might look like ...

Mapping the points of view of Joy, Heron, and the fisherman

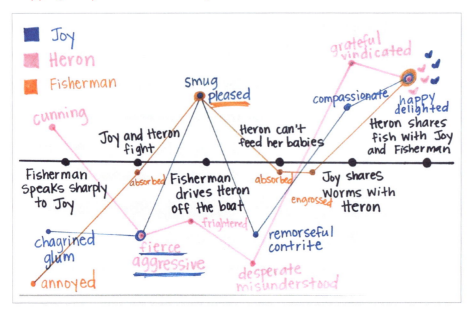

Mapear los puntos de vista de Joy, Heron y el pescador

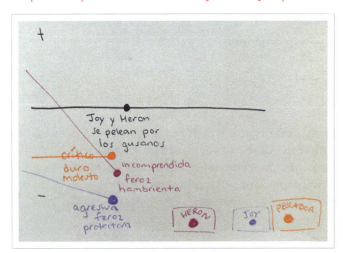

"Talking in Essay"

Considerations

Lesson summary: In this session you will engage students in "talking in essay," in which they defend a position or thesis about a character's traits or emotions, supporting that idea with evidence from the story. You'll demonstrate with an idea about Daniela from *Evelyn del Rey Is Moving Away*, and learners will practice expressing their ideas about Daniela, Joy, or Heron. You'll teach students a variety of academic transition phrases to help structure and extend their expression of ideas. Depending on the needs of your learning community, you might choose to showcase a sample essay beforehand to get students in the right mindset—either a written one or by "writing in the air."

This work gives learners more oral practice with literary vocabulary, and it integrates the academic language of transitional phrases into their literary discussions. It moves students from speaking in bullets to speaking in full paragraphs.

Estimated lesson time: 12 minutes.

Materials and preparation: You and students will need a "boxes and bullets" sketch of an essay structure, and sticky notes or a visual with academic transitional phrases. You and students will also need your word collections for Daniela and Joy and Heron, and your verticals.

Visit the website www.vocabularyconnections.org to download sample transitional phrase collections, in English and Spanish.

Additional lesson options: This work is fantastic preparation for literary essays, and also for coaching book club members to develop their ideas with text evidence. You might record students "talking in essay" as a celebration of their expressive language and interpretation skills, or you might invite students to flash-draft—write a quick draft on the heels of the idea they rehearsed orally. If you move into literary essays, work on their oral rehearsal, adding in academic transitions not only for leading into text evidence, but also for leading out. You'll find samples of transition charts in English and Spanish on the website www.vocabularyconnections.org.

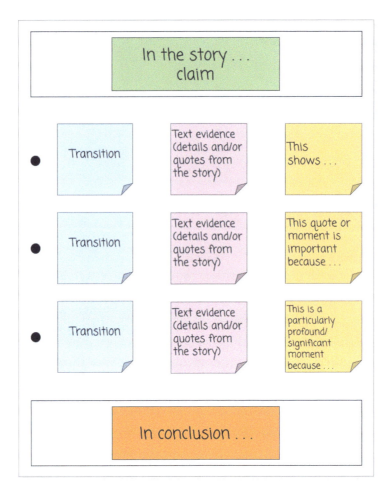

Launching the Lesson

Compliment learners on the ideas they have developed about characters, and how they are using their nuanced, precise literary vocabulary to express their ideas. Tell them that today you are going to help them practice with another word collection—transitional phrases. Have students take a moment to come up with an idea or two they want to explore.

You might say, "Readers, linguists, you've become expert at analyzing characters and expressing your ideas about their traits and emotions with precise literary vocabulary. Today you are going to practice 'talking in essay.' That's where you say your idea, you support it with evidence from the text, and you use transitional phrases to move from one example, to the next. You are going to be incredible at this, because you already have brilliant ideas, you know these texts so well, and you're an expert at paying attention to detail.

"You'll need two things to get started. One is a simple sketch—some people call it 'boxes and bullets,' others call it 'idea and evidence'—that will help you organize your thinking. Something that looks like this..."

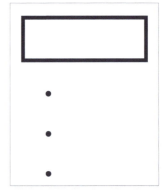

"The second thing you need is an idea about a character. You can choose Daniela, from *Evelyn del Rey Is Moving Away*, or Joy, or Heron, or even the fisherman. Then say an idea about one of their most important character traits or emotions. Like, maybe you are going to defend the idea that Joy is **protective**, or Heron is **misunderstood**. For example, I might say, 'My idea is that in the story, *Evelyn del Rey Is Moving Away*, Daniela is **sad**.' Then I'll talk about how in different scenes across the story, she is sad in different ways, and I'll use my literary vocabulary to describe that, showing how she is **worried** and **lonely** and **disconsolate**. Or I could talk about how in the beginning of the story Daniela is **excited** and **imaginative**, and at the end she is **lonely** and **inconsolable**."

Give learners a moment to think, then say, "What character could you talk about? What are some of your ideas? Do you want to talk about one trait or emotion, or a few? Tell your partner a few of your ideas."

As partners talk, you can voice over to help give them more ideas, and encouragement, saying, "Some of you want to talk about a few different emotions. Your thesis, or idea, then, might be that Joy is **volatile**—that means she changes a lot. Or you could say, 'Joy changes across the story. In the beginning …'"

Engagement—Sketchnoting and Literary Conversations

Demonstrate how to use the boxes and bullets outline to rehearse your oral essay. Role-play with students, where they play your partner, suggesting transitional phrases you can use from the tool you provide. Demonstrate how to add in transitional phrases. Then invite partners to give this a try.

You might say, "Watch me get started. You can be my partner. I'll use this box and bullet sketch to rehearse a simple essay. You suggest transitional phrases to help me. It might sound like … In the story, *Evelyn del Rey Is Moving Away*, Daniela is **sad**.

Now I want to move to my first example. What transitional phrases might I use? (Add in transitions as children call them out.) **For example, in the beginning of the story** Daniela worries that this is her last day with her best friend, her mejor amiga, Evelyn. Daniela is **sad** and **anxious**.

Now I want to move to my next example. What transitions can I use? I hear you … **Also, later in the story**, when Daniela is playing with Evelyn, even in the middle of her joy, she remembers Evelyn is leaving. She thinks about how she and her friend are the same and says, 'but not after today.' Daniela is **lonely**.

It's my last example, partners. What transitions should I use? I like your ideas … **In addition, near the end of the story**, as Evelyn gets in the car to leave, Daniela begins to cry—she is utterly **disconsolate**."

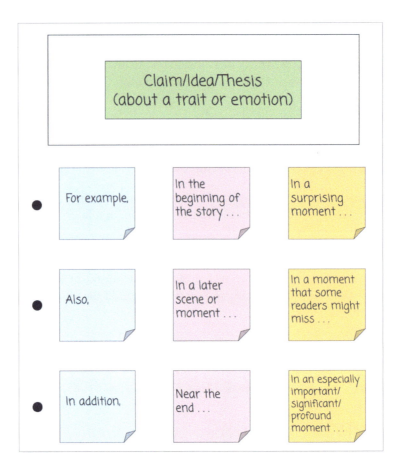

Recap, saying, "Do you see how as my partner, you prompted me to use transitions to develop the parts of my essay? Now you try. One partner will begin speaking in essay. The other partner can point to transitional phrases, and then the first partner has to try to add them in as they speak."

You can extend this work, offering essayists ways to structure their oral essay, as times when/ways or kinds/reasons. These simple structures help novice essayists talk and write with structure—especially helpful if you are pairing this work with literary essay writing.

You might say, "Essayists! You just said a whole essay out loud. I'm going to show you one more tool that you can use, to organize your essay into parts. Go back to your boxes and bullets sketch. Now imagine that you are going to not only have examples, but parts to your essay. You could divide your essay into 'times when,' which we just did. But you could also try dividing your essay into ways or kinds, or reasons.

For example, mine might sound like, **One way** that Daniela is **sad** is she is **worried**. **For example, in the beginning of the story** … Then I might say … **Another way** Daniela is sad is she is lonely. **For example, in the middle of the story** … and then I might end with … **A final way** Daniela is **sad** is she is **disconsolate** … **For example, near the end of the story** … Or I could try reasons. **One reason** Daniela is sad is because …"

Invite students to try. "You try. It might be that your essay sounds best as 'times when.' But try organizing it as reasons or ways or kinds."

Application

Celebrate the work students have done, not just in this lesson, but in all the lessons, learning literary vocabulary, applying it in context, developing nuanced ideas and language.

"Readers, you have done some incredible work across these lessons. You've learned so much literary vocabulary and done such insightful interpretation work. Pat yourself on the back! Tell your partner a favorite word or two! Remember, this is work that doesn't just apply to Joy and Heron, or to Daniela. Whenever you are analyzing characters, you can reach for precise, expressive language. Well done!"

The work students will create during and after the lesson might look like ...

Algunos transiciones

Some sophisticated transitional phrases

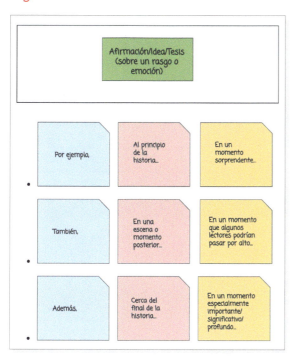

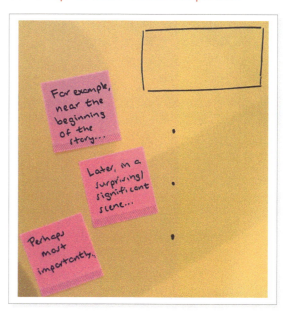

An anchor chart helps learners remember and transfer skills and habits

Readers Deepen Literary Vocabulary ♡

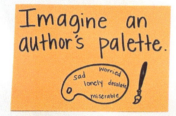

Imagine an author's palette.

Make an emotional timeline.

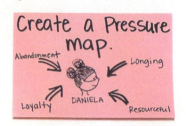

Create a Pressure map.

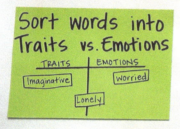

Sort words into Traits vs. Emotions

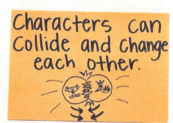

Characters can Collide and change each other.

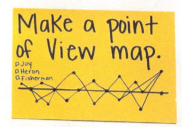

Make a point of View map.

Support ideas with evidence from the story.

Part

II

Word Consciousness

Chapter 3

Building Word Consciousness Through Etymology

The Scope of These Lessons— What's Going to Happen!

The word *inculcate* means to instill an attitude, idea, or habit through persistent instruction. This is what we'll work toward across the lessons in this chapter and the next—to instill an attitude of curiosity, the idea that words are fascinating and have histories you can investigate, and the habit of figuring out meanings and creating new words using word knowledge.

You'll begin with a lesson on *etymology*—the linguistic ancestry of English. I often show an historical timeline and a map to help children conceptualize where England is, and to help them visualize the role of invasion, occupation, and colonialism in influencing language development.

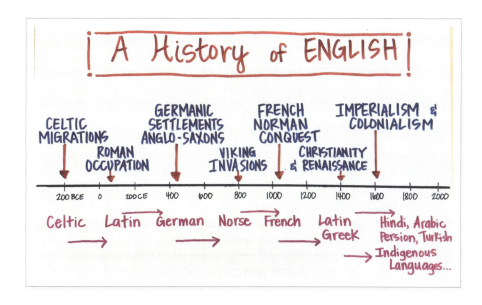

It's important to also talk about how English, like all languages, not only developed in the past, but it is still developing, simultaneously and distinctly around the planet. This generation of children will learn English words that we did not know, in the same way our parents' generation learned words like **computer** and **internet** over time. Youngsters speaking English in Mumbai, India, will know and create English words that are different from those known and created by children in San Diego, California.

Children like to learn about history and language. They like to learn about word parts and to see them in what they are reading. It's important, as well, to teach about the multiplicity of sources for the English language, including Indigenous sources, and the linguistic crossover that happens with colonization. This might be as simple as inviting learners to think about the implications of the etymology of the Anglo-Saxon words: **cow, chicken, pig**, and the Norman-French words: **beef, poultry, pork**. The conquered Anglo-Saxon farmers raise the animals; the ruling Norman courtiers order meals. You might invite learners to think of all the Spanish words that have made their way into English: **rodeo, patio, mosquito, macho**, and so on. Or you might invite learners to consider the impact of colonialism as they explore the significance of English words that were absorbed from Indigenous languages, such as: **chocolate, potato, hammock, kayak, chipmunk**. Remember that you and your students can turn to AI to explore language crossover.

Teaching that names matter also … matters. Understanding that the **Haudenosaunee** choose and ask to be called by their self-designated name, meaning "people of the longhouse" instead of **Iroquois**, a name that was laid on them by competitors and enemies, matters. Learning that **Mumbai** used to be called **Bombay** and was renamed as an act of liberation and reclamation, or that the very peoples who gave Chicago its name were then forcibly relocated to not live there, is a lesson in the metaphoric quality of names as identity markers and power struggles. This is a vocabulary book, not a book on teaching critical social studies and ethical civics (spend some time with *The Civically Engaged Classroom* (2020), for more on that!), so there is only one lesson in this chapter on names, but it's important because vocabulary words often reflect histories of power. The youngest children know this, through their own experience with name-calling. They know the difference between choosing what you are called and being called something by others. Even one lesson on names and their history can instill the notion that language is not neutral, encouraging raised awareness.

From *etymology*, you'll move to *cognates*, which you may have already introduced in lessons from prior chapters. Here, you'll invite students to practice recognizing and figuring out the meaning of cognates, giving them a bunch of words to sort. The goal is not for children to memorize these cognates. It is to deepen their awareness of cognates, both so they can extend their word recognition across languages, and so they become more conscious of the crossover of language (Carlo et al., 2004; Cenoz, Leonet, and Gorter, 2022; Helman, 2016). This kind of cognitive flexibility will help their word consciousness in all languages.

Later lessons in this chapter focus on *compound words*. You'll teach learners about:

- *closed compounds* (combinations that are written as one word, such as **sunflower, snowman**)

- *hyphenated compounds* (combinations connected by a hyphen, such as **third-grade, part-time**)

- *open compounds* (combinations written as two words such as **ice cream, high school**)

You'll engage students in games like Blank Slate, where they create compound words from one part of a word (**fire_____** creates **firefly, fire truck, fireworks**) and Compound Connection Challenge where they try to derive a list of compounds, building from an initial word.

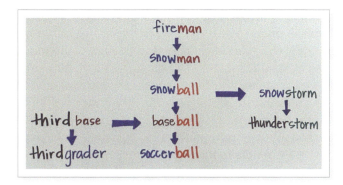

Learning Goals

Expect your learners to become sensitive to the history of words and where they come from. Expect them to wonder and critique how power and colonialism shapes names of people, groups, and places. Expect them to become curious about word choice. Expect them to begin to recognize compound words and better grasp their meaning in what they read. Learning about compound words also helps students develop more flexible thinking and creativity in how they approach words.

Here are some specific learning goals that are built into this work.

- To deepen students' consciousness of etymology—an appreciation for linguistic ancestry.

- To promote critical thinking and curiosity about history and language.

- To gain insight into how names reflect power, history, choice, and identity.

- To expand vocabulary directly with knowledge of compound words.

- To expand learners' flexibility in figuring out the meaning of new compound words.

Text Recommendations

Unlike the vocabulary collecting and application of Chapter 1 and Chapter 2, these lessons will mostly include direct instruction, with some inquiry and games. You'll teach children a bit of knowledge (such as a brief history of English), and engage them in applying that knowledge. So you won't necessarily showcase a read-aloud text to anchor this work. That said, you'll notice a synergistic effect if you engage students in transferring their word consciousness with texts on hand, including ones you demonstrate during read-aloud or shared reading, and the books children are reading.

It is lovely to have a familiar text readily available to show children examples of how increased word consciousness leads us to notice more about the vocabulary in what we are reading—and helps us figure out likely meanings of words. For example, in the first page of *Evelyn Rey Is Moving Away*, Daniela describes her "**número uno**" best friend—an opportunity to highlight cognates and how they help learners figure out unfamiliar vocabulary. Later, Daniela explains how they play "**hide-and-seek**," an opportunity to highlight hyphenated compounds. Just after that she describes imagining "**bus stops**" and "**skyscrapers**," which are great for demonstrating an open compound and a closed compound. The main goal here is to demonstrate how word consciousness changes what you notice as you read.

You can also introduce a new text to accompany the lessons in this chapter (and the next). If you have time for a new read-aloud, I recommend *My Papi Has a Motorcycle* (2019), written by Isabel Quintero and illustrated by Zeke Peña. It is chock full of compounds, cognates, and morphologically interesting vocabulary. And it is a gorgeous, significant story of a daughter's love for her father, her place, her culture, and her history. The translanguaging demonstrates the entwining of cultures and languages, and the exploration of Daisy's neighborhood suggests important motifs of history, place, and belonging. You can, of course, bring in other texts that are your favorites, that feel important to you and your students. The beautiful thing about word consciousness is that the vocabulary in any text becomes more intriguing once you bring more awareness to it.

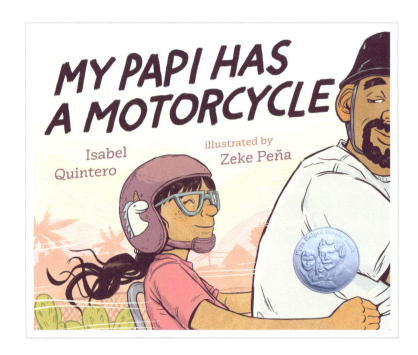

Opportunities for Transfer and Application

You should see and foster transfer and application of students' increased word knowledge in their reading comprehension and in their writing. As readers, your multilingual students will notice more cognates. All your readers can use their knowledge of compound words to apply flexible strategies to figuring out more words in the texts they read. Similarly, encourage your students to bring their new word knowledge and creativity to their writing. You might create an anchor chart as a reminder of the different ways students are becoming word conscious.

An anchor chart helps learners remember and transfer skills and habits

If you are able, occasionally, to teach these lessons just prior to children spending some time reading, they'll often immediately transfer their knowledge, noticing and collecting words that relate to what you just taught.

Studying etymology and compound words intersects especially well with:

- independent reading

- social studies

- test prep

- narrative and nonfiction writing

- intervention groups

- enrichment groups

Assessment Options

There are simple assessments you can give to grasp children's increasing word consciousness, including matching exercises and word building games. The goal of all of these lessons is really to increase students' curiosity about and knowledge of how words work overall. You'll also want to pay attention, therefore, to children's attitude toward words. Celebrate when they bring a new word to the class's attention. Create word charts to capture investigations. Invite students to collect words related to your instruction. Some possibilities for assessment include:

- *Word Conscious Collectors.* Invite learners to collect words from their independent reading that match your instruction, such as compound words or cognates.

- *Combinations for Compounds.* Provide learners with word cards and ask them to create as many compounds as they can.

Links to Standards

Reading Anchor Standard 4: Interpret words and phrases as they are used in a text, including determining technical, connotative, and figurative meanings, and analyze how specific word choices shape meaning or tone.

Language Anchor Standard 4: Determine or clarify the meaning of unknown and multiple-meaning words and phrases by using context clues, analyzing meaningful word parts, and consulting general and specialized reference materials, as appropriate.

Language Anchor Standard 5: Demonstrate understanding of figurative language, word relationships and nuances in word meanings.

Lesson 3.1

Etymology Excitement

Considerations

Lesson summary: In this session you will teach students a bit about the history of the English language, showing them a map and timeline. You'll give a micro-lecture, tucking in examples of words and their ancestry. (It's tricky to keep this short and accessible—lean on the visuals!) Then you'll invite learners to study words from around the world that have made their way into English. If you're comfortable using technology, you'll find plenty of words from a variety of languages or places that have made their way into English, giving you more opportunities to celebrate English as a changing language as well as the cultural and linguistic histories of your community (España and Yadira Herrera, 2020). Your AI partner can suggest words, and give you details of derivation and meaning, which are fascinating.

This work familiarizes students with the depth and breadth of sources of English. It stimulates their word consciousness and their alertness to how language grows and changes. By celebrating words from many linguistic sources, you also deepen the cultural bonds in your community.

Estimated lesson time: 10 minutes.

Materials and preparation: You'll display a map and a timeline of the history of English. Visit the website www.vocabularyconnections.org to download a sample map and timeline.

You'll also need access to AI or the internet. One choice is for you to access AI, with kids making suggestions. Another is for you to set your students up with EdTech AI such as SchoolAI that lets your students research easily. Or you can research this information beforehand, using your knowledge of your students to create an inclusive community list that students can study and add to.

Additional lesson options: A great extension for this lesson is to create a linguistic map of your classroom community that celebrates children's cultural and linguistic histories. You can overlay the words you discover in your etymology investigation on this map, adding more words over time.

Launching the Lesson

Teach students a bit about the history of the English language, using a timeline and map to help show them some of the major influences of English. Teach the word **etymology**.

You might say, "Today you are **linguists** and **etymologists**! A **linguist** is someone who studies languages, and an **etymologist** studies the history of language. English is one of the most complicated languages, because it has been influenced by so many other languages over its history. Let me show you a map, so you can see where English started. It was on this small island, called ... England!"

Then you might show a timeline as well, pointing out some of the highlights, saying, "Let's look at this timeline too. You can see here how first there were Celtic people on the land, and then the Romans invaded. Some of their original Roman-Latin words have stuck, like **wall**. Then came the Anglo-Saxons, who first invaded and then stayed and settled across England. They spoke an early form of German, and they brought new, Germanic words like **man**. Then the Vikings invaded, and they brought **Norse** words, like the word **knife**. And then the French invaded, and they brought French, which is a language very heavily based on Latin. They brought new words like **court**. They also brought the Christian church with them, which brought more Greek and Latin. So many influences!"

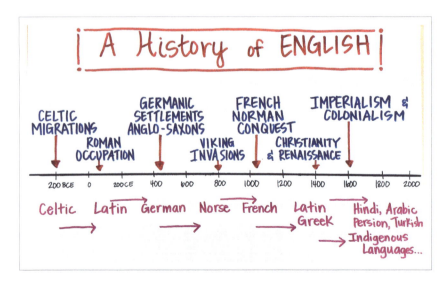

Engagement—Word Investigations

Engage students in studying English words that have derived from other languages (especially those represented in your community). Students can also seek more words from other places. (You can use Google or use SchoolAI, or another generative AI platform, to conduct some searches.)

You might say, "The amazing thing about language is, it not only has a history, it has a future. It continues to grow. Words from all around the world have made their way into English. I've got a list here with some words from other languages and places. Study it with your partner. If you know other words, add them with a sticky note! And we can use technology to find more!"

khaki	Urdu and Persian
taekwando	Korean
shampoo	Hindi
typhoon	Chinese
patio	Spanish
borchst	Ukranian
algebra	Arabic
boondocks	Filipino & Tagalog
cafe	French
tsar or csar	Russian

Application

Encourage students to be alert to words from other languages as they read, and to research the languages that are part of their family history and culture.

You might say, "Let's keep this up, linguists! If you find new words from other places and languages that have drifted into English, add them to our chart! And find out more about the languages that are part of your family history!"

The work students will create during or after the lesson might look like ...

A classroom community linguistic map

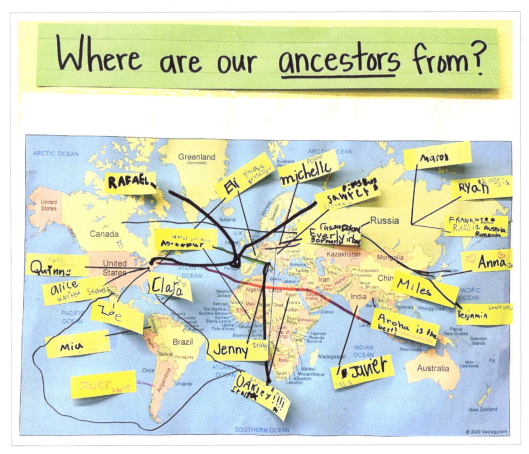

Finding German words that have crossed over into English

Using SchoolAI as a partner to explore linguistic heritage

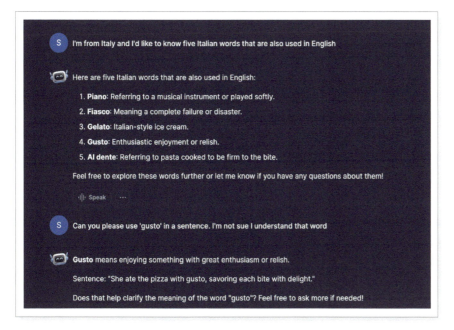

S I'm from Italy and I'd like to know five Italian words that are also used in English

🤖 Here are five Italian words that are also used in English:

1. **Piano**: Referring to a musical instrument or played softly.
2. **Fiasco**: Meaning a complete failure or disaster.
3. **Gelato**: Italian-style ice cream.
4. **Gusto**: Enthusiastic enjoyment or relish.
5. **Al dente**: Referring to pasta cooked to be firm to the bite.

Feel free to explore these words further or let me know if you have any questions about them!

⫿⫿ Speak   ···

S Can you please use 'gusto' in a sentence. I'm not sue I understand that word

🤖 **Gusto** means enjoying something with great enthusiasm or relish.

Sentence: "She ate the pizza with gusto, savoring each bite with delight."

Does that help clarify the meaning of the word "gusto"? Feel free to ask more if needed!

Names Matter

Considerations

Lesson summary: In this session you'll introduce the idea that names matter. For students of any age, one of the most important ideas is that people prefer to choose their own names, and that some historical names reflect histories of oppression. For example, names given to groups of people by outsiders, such as **gypsy, Iroquois, Eskimo**, were all given by competitors and colonizers and reflect cultural misunderstandings and stereotypes. A second part of this idea is that place names, too, reflect complicated histories of power and occupation. Today, you'll introduce this idea, share some examples, and then give students a little time to research and talk about the linguistic histories of a few names that have worked their way into our collective vocabulary.

This work emphasizes for children that names matter, and that we can ask respectful questions about what people want to be called, as well as how events in history and power differences have shaped names.

Estimated lesson time: 10–15 minutes.

Materials and preparation: You'll need information on the history of a few names to share. Learners can use Google, or you can set them up with a generative AI space such as SchoolAI. Alternatively, if time is short, you can access name cards with some examples at the link provided. You can invite students to discuss them in partnerships— the new names they learn and what they learn about how names often reflect shifting histories of power. Remember that AI can be your partner, and you can easily look up local histories of people and places that will be especially relevant to your learning community.

Visit the website www.vocabularyconnections.org to download printable name cards.

Additional lesson options: If you also teach social studies, you can engage students in a decolonizing "remapping" project, in which they layer original Indigenous names for people and places over a current map. You can also teach students how to investigate their local geography, asking: What peoples have lived here? What place names have changed over time? Are there any place names that reflect Indigenous presence and language?

In a writing workshop, giving students a chance to do some freewriting about moments when they or others have been name-called, and/or what it means to choose your own name, can be a powerful entry into narrative or personal essay writing. Children might also explore the history of their own name.

Launching the Lesson

Teach students a little bit about how names reflect histories and cultures. Start with an example of Anglo-Saxon words for farm animals, and Norman-French words for cooked food, a comparison that reflects social classes in the Middle Ages.

You might say, "Linguists! Today you're going to learn something important you can do when you are studying words. That is, you can ask questions about *names*—names of things, names of people, names of places. Because often, when new people sweep in and invade and occupy the land, the occupiers bring new words for things. Let me give you an example. Remember we learned yesterday that when the Normans invaded England, they became the rulers, the aristocracy. They brought French with them. The Anglo-Saxon farmers kept speaking Anglo-Saxon. But gradually English began to include words from both languages. I'm going to show you a list of words, and let's see what we notice. You can go ahead and whisper to your partner, if you have some ideas."

Anglo-Saxon	Norman-French
Cow	Beef
Chicken	Poultry
Pig	Pork
Deer	Venison
Egg	Omelet

Then you might add, "It's interesting, right? If you were ordering a servant to cook a meal, you wouldn't say, 'I want a **cow** for dinner.' You'd say, 'Let's have **beef**.' Or you might say, 'I'd like an **omelet**.' Notice how these different words reflect power and rank. The Anglo-Saxon farmers raised animals, and the Norman rulers ordered meals."

Engagement—Word Investigations

Suggest that the names of people and places especially give you insight into histories of power. Give students an opportunity to research and discuss local place names and names of peoples who resided nearby, or use the downloadable name cards as sources of discussion.

You might say, "Linguists, there are two kinds of names that often reflect things that have happened in history—that is names of people and names of places. As you can imagine, when the Romans invaded England, they renamed many places. That's how **London** got its name. The Romans named it **Londinium**. So the name reflects the Roman conquest of the Celts. Whereas when the Anglo-Saxons invaded, they named cities with Anglo-Saxon names, like **Oxford**. And when the Normans invaded, they named cities with French names, like **Richmond**. I have some cards with the histories of some names of people and places. You can study them with your partner, and talk about what new ideas you have about the significance of names in history."

Application

Suggest that it's always respectful to try to find out what people want to be called, and to be aware that names often reflect complicated histories of power.

You might say, "Researchers, linguists, you have a lot of insights about how names can reflect histories of power. Stay alert to this, so you can ask respectful questions about what people want to be called. You can also investigate how the names that have been given to people or places reflect who was in power."

The work students will create during and after the lesson might look like ...

Using SchoolAI to research local place names

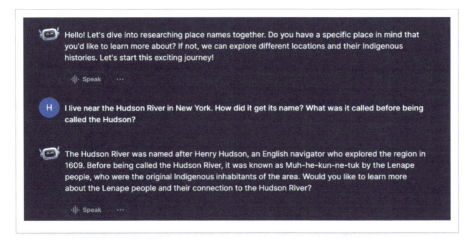

Students in Marc Todd's classroom remap Indigenous people's presence onto a U.S. road map—renaming as a decolonizing practice

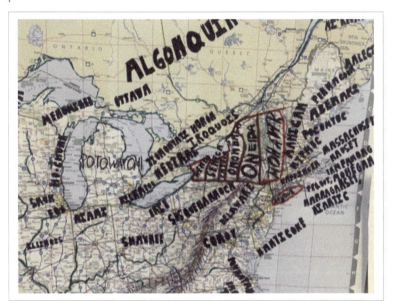

Cognate Connections

Considerations

Lesson summary: In this session you will continue to explore etymology, this time exploring *cognates*, which are words that descend from the same ancestral language. You'll begin by explaining (or reviewing) what cognates are and giving some examples of how being alert to cognates can extend vocabulary knowledge across languages. Then you'll give students an opportunity to do some rapid sorts of cognates, inviting them to notice spelling patterns as well.

This work helps many of your multilingual learners, as it can help comprehension, vocabulary acquisition, and language transfer. Knowing that most Spanish words that end in "dad" become the same word ending in "ty" in English is hugely helpful! This work can help all your students become more aware of cognate similarities, so they can boost their awareness of vocabulary across languages.

Estimated lesson time: 10 minutes.

Materials and preparation: You'll need a list of cognates that you can cut up so that students can sort them. Visit the website www.vocabularyconnections.org to download cognate lists.

Additional lesson options: As an extension, you might engage students in figuring out the likely meaning of a few sentences in unfamiliar languages, using visual images with sentences including cognates. Visit the website www. vocabularyconnections.org to download visual images for students to practice deciphering cognates. You can also encourage students to use AI to explore cognates in non-Romance languages.

Launching the Lesson

Remind students of what they already know about cognates, and invite them to notice any patterns in an example.

You might say, "Linguists, you probably remember what **cognates** are. **Cognates** are words that sound similar, and have similar meanings, across languages. You get the most cognates between languages that share similar roots. Portuguese, Spanish, Italian, French, and English all have strong Latin roots, so there are many cognates. But there are also cognates between English and German, and between English and Russian.

"When you study cognates, you're studying patterns—and you look at what's the same, and sometimes what tends to change a little bit. Join me in trying that now. Here are some cognates in English and Spanish. Talk with your partner—do you notice any pattern? Do you have any theories?"

Education	Educación
Attention	Atención
Impression	Impresión
Compassion	Compasión

Engagement—Word Investigations

Debrief patterns in what you studied together, and give partnerships some cognate collections to sort, study, and talk about.

You might say, "You noticed that it seems like words that end in 'tion' in English, seem to end in 'ción' in Spanish. Some of you have a theory that words that have double consonants, like tt or ss, become a single consonant in Spanish. That's worth investigating!"

Then set children up to investigate further. You might say, "Take an envelope with your partner. There are a bunch of words in English, French, and Spanish in the envelope. See what happens when you sort these into cognate collections. What patterns do you notice? What theories do you have? What words do you learn!?"

Application

Encourage children to be alert to cognates as a way to learn more about language, and to learn languages.

You might say, "Learning to study cognates will expand your vocabulary, and help you with languages you are learning now or in the future. Be alert to them, not just in these languages, but in any language. When the characters in the books you are reading speak in different languages, look for cognates as a way to figure out the meaning of new words!"

The work students will create during and after the lesson might look like ...

Sorting a cognate collection

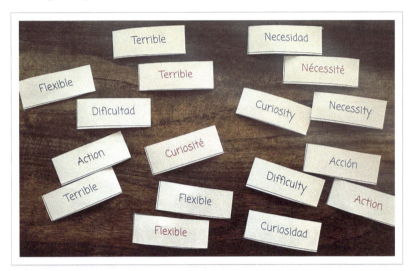

Cognates of al-jabr

Cognate detectives decipher meaning

Elle est superbe!

Lesson 3.4

Compound Collections

Considerations

Lesson summary: In this session you'll teach students about the different kinds of compounds, including *closed*, *hyphenated*, and *open* compounds. You'll engage children in an inquiry to help them figure out what compound words are, then you'll invite students to figure out the meaning of compound vocabulary words by using their knowledge of smaller words inside the large compounds.

This work will make your students more aware of and flexible with reading, deciphering, and writing compound words. Understanding compound words helps children figure out the meanings of unfamiliar words by breaking them down into smaller, recognizable parts. Knowledge of compound words also aids spelling proficiency. By understanding how words are constructed, children can spell compound words more accurately. This work also encourages creativity and word play. Children love to experiment with combining words to create their own compound words, fostering linguistic creativity.

Estimated lesson time: 8 minutes.

Materials and preparation: You'll need two things for this lesson. First, a small list of compound words of each type, for students to investigate during the lesson. Second, a group of compound words with which students can practice deciphering meaning. You can choose among easier or harder lists, and you may give learners different lists based on your knowledge of your students.

Visit the website www.vocabularyconnections.org to download compound word lists, as well as visual tools for multilingual learners.

Additional lesson options: Compound words are significant in all aspects of literacy. You might extend this lesson in your writing instruction, teaching children to use their knowledge of compound words to both improve their spelling and reach for more complex vocabulary in their writing. You'll definitely want to teach children to use their knowledge of compound words as they read, to figure out the meaning of new words from smaller, familiar parts. For multilingual learners, you might engage them in an inquiry, gathering compound words in more than one language. **Palabras compuestas** are common in Spanish, for instance, as are **komposita** in German, **mots composés** in French, or **합성어** in Korean.

Launching the Lesson

Introduce the concept of compound words, inviting children to theorize from some examples. Then explain their types (closed, hyphenated, open), giving examples of each.

You might say, "Linguists, today you'll investigate a new group of words. They are called compound words, and I bet you can figure out what compound words are from these examples. Whisper to your partner—what theories do you have as you study these words?"

backpack	video game	cowboy
self-esteem	living room	starfish

To explain the types of compound words, you might say, "You figured out that compound words are made from two smaller words, and together they make a new word. The meaning of that new word is related to the smaller words, so you'll be able to figure out SO MANY new words when you understand compounds! You're probably noticing different types of compound words here. When the two words become one word, that's a closed compound, like **cowboy**. Or it can be hyphenated, like **self-esteem**. An open compound has a space, like **living room**. It's not important to remember what these are called. What matters is that you can create compound words in these three ways."

Including images for multilingual learners will deepen engagement and understanding

Engagement—Word Investigations

Engage students in a game—figuring out the meaning of compound words, using their knowledge of smaller, recognizable word parts.

You might say, "Let's play a game. To play this game, you and your partner will see how many new vocabulary words you can figure out, because you know the meaning of the small words inside. Some are easier, and some will be harder—do your best. Use your knowledge of smaller words to figure out these bigger words. Ready … see how many words you can figure out with your partner!"

lighthouse	dress shoes	firefly
bugspray	grandparents	teammate
brother-in-law	full moon	eco-friendly
bittersweet	coffee table	waterproof

Application

Encourage students to use the strategy of figuring out compound words from their knowledge of smaller words in their reading, and to be extra alert to compound words as they read.

You might say, "Linguists! Recognizing compound words will be a super power for you as you are reading. When you see a word you think might be a compound word, ask yourself—can I figure out what this vocabulary word means, because I know the meaning of the smaller words inside it?"

The work students will create during and after the lesson might look like ...

Readers collect compound words—visible signs of word consciousness!

These students figure out the smaller words inside of compound words

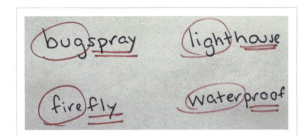

These students study *palabras compuestas* in Spanish

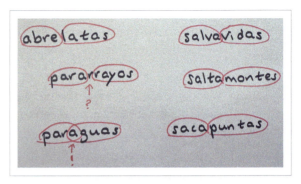

Exploring compounds that are also cognates!

Compound Creators

Considerations

Lesson summary: In this session you'll remind learners of what they've learned about compound works, and teach that they can create new compound words from smaller words they know. You'll engage students in creating vocabulary words with a partner.

This work supports children's linguistic and cognitive development. By combining known words to form new ones, children can express more complex ideas. Also, the process of forming compound words requires children to engage in linguistic analysis, enhancing their problem-solving skills and ability to manipulate language. Recognizing that compound words are made up of smaller, familiar units can make challenging words less intimidating as well—in reading and writing.

Estimated lesson time: 8 minutes.

Materials and preparation: You'll need a collection of small words from which to make large words. You might supply an easier set, with visual cues, for multilingual learners. You can simply display the words, or print them out and cut them up, so children can manipulate them. Visit the website www.vocabularyconnections.org to download printable word collections and visual tools.

Additional lesson options: A clear extension to this lesson arises in writing instruction, where you can teach children to apply their knowledge of making compounds to use more complex vocabulary and spell it accurately. Another possible extension could be an investigation of meaning shifts. Compound words sometimes carry specific meanings that differ from the meanings of their individual components. You might explore these semantic shifts with students, sorting compound words into categories of "closely matching the smaller words they stem from," like **raincoat** and "drifting from original meaning." Some examples of the latter include **butterfly, eavesdrop, deadline, blackmail**. It's interesting to ask an AI partner to supply the etymology of words like these. The main goal is for children to become ever more word conscious.

Launching the Lesson

Remind children of what they know about compound words, and the different kinds of compounds, giving some examples.

You might say, "Linguists! You know about the history of words, you know about cognates, and now you know about compounds. Let's work through a quick reminder. Here are some compound words—tell your partner, what are the different kinds of compounds?"

| Ice cream | self-esteem | backpack |

You might add, "Compound words come in different forms—you might make ones that are *open*, where there is a space between the two words, like **ice cream**. Or you might use a hyphen, like in **self-esteem**. Or you can stick them together, as in **backpack**. The main thing to notice is that you can make new, bigger words, from smaller, simpler words."

Teach students they can not only figure out the meaning of compound words, they can also create them, using smaller words they know. Demonstrate, inviting learners to share their ideas as you do so. You might invite learners to try figuring out a compound in a new language as well.

You might say, "Linguists, you know that you can figure out the meaning of lots of compound words, or get close to the meaning, from the smaller words you know. For instance, knowing that ice is frozen and cream is made of milk, I can figure out that ice cream is probably like frozen milk—which it is! And you can also create new words! For example, let's imagine I know the meaning of **book** and **shelf**. I can make ... **bookshelf**."

book   shelf   bookshelf

Engagement—Word Investigations

Engage students in creating compound words from smaller, familiar words. Supply students with some "starter" words, and encourage them to add new ones they know.

Invite children to play a linguistic game—Compound Creator. You might say, "Let's give you a chance to try this. Here are some starter words—see how many new words you can make with a partner!"

snow	storm	man	team
strike	base	mate	bug
foot	soul	truck	ball
fire	lightning	lady	soccer

Celebrate students' work, and elevate it as well. You might say, "So many new words! **Lightning strike** and **football** and **snow storm** and **ladybug**! And this one is creative— **football team**! That one is made up of three words!"

Application

Encourage learners to continue this word game on their own, and to use this knowledge of how to build words when they are writing. Also encourage them to use these strategies in all their languages.

You might say, "You have super powers now! You can build new, bigger words, from smaller words you know. And you can try this in all your languages. Remember this strategy, when you are writing!"

The work students will create during and after the lesson might look like ...

Creating multiple vocabulary words using *foot*

Palabras compuestas

Multilingual learners play with images to make new words

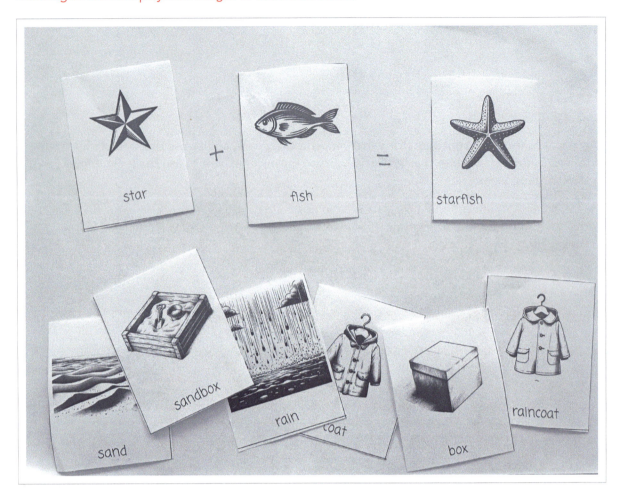

Word Games

Considerations

Lesson summary: In this session you'll teach your learners two word games. The first is based on a game called Blank Slate that students can also take home to play with family and friends! In the game, one player chooses a card, and every player makes a compound word from it. There are a couple of scoring methods, including ones that are very collaborative and relaxed and others that are more rapid and competitive. Children can choose the version that will give them joy.

The second game is a Compound Connection Challenge. In this game, one player jots a word, and each team tries to create a list of compounds, each one needing one part from the word before. There can be various rules—the game can be scored (a point for each word), or just played to create long lists, and it can be played by teams or in partnerships. For example:

fireman

snowman

snowball

baseball

You can make this game easier by providing word cards as starter sets.

Estimated lesson time: 10 minutes.

Materials and preparation: You'll need a description of the rules of each game— you may decide to provide different versions. The same word cards that launch Blank Slate can launch Compound Relay. You can also add in some words in other languages that you know students speak, so that teammates lean on and appreciate their community's linguistic competencies. It can be helpful to provide teams with sticky notes and chart paper so that after they create their word collections you can display and celebrate them. Visit the website www.vocabularyconnections.org to download word cards in English and Spanish as well as scoring cards.

Additional lesson options: Children can play variations of this game in other languages—you can use AI to generate word cards. They can also combine picture cards to make new words. And they can make their own versions of Blank Slate, creating word cards themselves.

Launching the Lesson

Explain the games, handing out simple rule cards to teams.

You might say, "Linguists are people who love words and know a lot about them. You are definitely becoming linguists! You already know more about words than most adults! Today you'll have a chance to play some word games, to sharpen your linguistic skills. You can play these in teams or partnerships. You can play Blank Slate. In this game, teams make compound words from a single word, and there is a scoring system. Or you can play Compound Connection Challenge, where you and your partner or team try to make as many linked compounds as you can. I have the rules here for you."

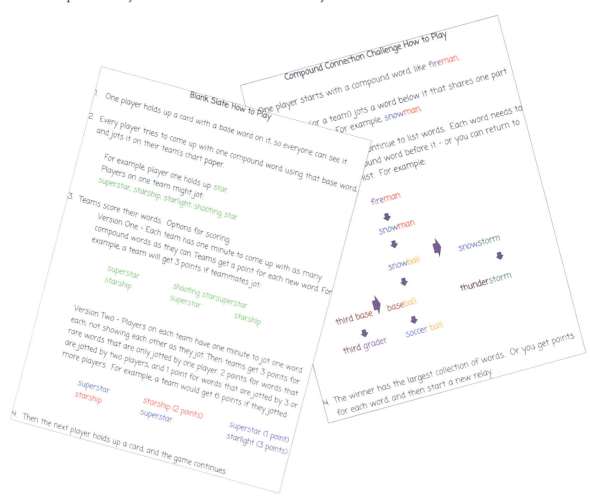

Engagement—Word Investigations

Invite students to play. You may have to do some strategic social engineering to make sure that children have partners and teams they enjoy, and play the kind of game (fast and competitive, or simply creative and collaborative) that they enjoy.

It matters that when children play games, they feel secure, not threatened. Some children love competition, others abhor it. Some children get excited with a timer; others fall apart when they see it. As you talk to children, you might say things like:

"I've been thinking about you, and I bet you'd like to play this creatively with a partner, without scoring to slow you down—you can see how many words you create together, moving to a new base word when you feel like you've done as much as you can. Here's a piece of chart paper—let's see you fill it up!"

Or

"This game is fun in teams—then you can support each other. I've even thrown in a few base words in different languages—so you can lean on all your teammates' languages!"

Or

"Get ready, players. This is a sharp competition, and it's timed! It will go fast, and you'll win some rounds and not others. The main thing is, your brain will be on fire!"

Application

Share some of the lists, creation and successes. Encourage children to play these games with family and friends, in any language. Remind them of how their brains are growing all the time, and these kinds of games will light up new growth in their brains!

You might say, "Linguistic champions, all of you! Look at some of these word lists from Compound Connection, and collections from Blank Slate! Look at the compound words in more than one language! Pat yourself on the back! Now, players, I want to let you into a secret. Your brain is literally growing while you play these games. Just like when you play soccer, or piano, you strengthen your legs and fingers when you play these games, you strengthen the part of your brain that remembers and deciphers words! So, play these with family and friends! We can make sets so you can take them home."

The work students will create during and after the lesson might look like ...

These players create multiple lists of compounds in their Compound Connection game

Students can also create their own versions of Blank Slate

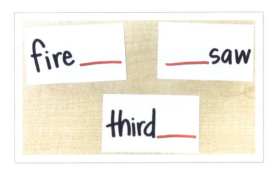

An anchor chart helps learners remember and transfer skills and habits

Morphology Investigations

The Scope of These Lessons— What's Going to Happen!

The lessons in this chapter focus on *morphology*—teaching common prefixes and suffixes, and a few roots, so that when learners encounter a new word with one of these, they can decipher its meaning, or at least its connotation, because they know something about morphemes, or the parts of words. Even very young readers benefit from learning morphology. This word consciousness makes your readers more linguistically flexible, so that they are better able to decipher or approximate the meaning of many words (Sedita, 2018; Shanahan, 2018). English is a language with many origins, and only about half of English words have their origins in Greek and Latin roots and affixes (prefixes and suffixes). But half is a lot, and once you know that **re** generally means **back** or **again**, that knowledge can help you figure out the probable meaning of words like **rewrite, reread, redo, reexamine, rebuild, reorganize**, and so on.

Each morphology lesson here follows a protocol, so that you can teach all the prefixes, suffixes, and roots you want, following this same protocol. You can download the protocol from the website www.vocabularyconnections.org, and it is described in each lesson.

There are many prefixes and suffixes and roots, and teachers often wonder about which ones to teach in which grades. In his blogpost, "What Should Morphology Instruction Look Like," Tim Shanahan says that he doesn't know of any particular list of morphemes (the smallest part of a word that carries meaning) that should be taught at any grade (Shanahan, 2018). In that same blogpost, Peter Bowers says that he also wouldn't recommend such a list. Instead, he suggests following up as students come upon words, so that the class inquiry responds to words that learners encounter in the texts they are reading. I love the idea of building on student interest, and Tim includes a fabulous video of a classroom teacher doing that with second graders. *And* I like the idea of planning to teach morphology in a cohesive way, so I generally do begin with a list, while welcoming conversations around morphemes students bring to the class's attention.

If you're like me and prefer to start with an anchor list in hand while, at the same time, leaving room to follow your students' inquiries, I think the best starter list to

help teachers plan which morphemes to teach is the "Multi-year Plan for Systematic Morphology Instruction" that Cunningham, Burkins, and Yates share in their downloadables to accompany their book, *Shifting the Balance: Six Ways to Bring the Science of Reading into the Upper Grade Classroom, 3–5*. Their plan suggests a few prefixes and suffixes, for example, to teach in grade 3, and a few more, plus some roots, to teach in grades 4–5. And there is an extra list of "other useful morphemes" which would make great instruction in grade 6. It is simply super.

The main thing to note in terms of instruction is that students respond very well to a protocol for learning morphemes. They enjoy the sense of ritual, they participate with a sense of confidence because they quickly become familiar with the blend of direct instruction and inquiry, and they can help shape the lesson by suggesting kinesthetic actions for each morpheme. These lessons are fast, highly participatory, engaging, and effective. And they are replicable. You can repeat the prefix lesson, for instance, to teach each prefix on your instructional list. You can repeat the suffix lesson to teach each suffix on your list. And you can repeat the root lesson to teach each root you decide to tackle. Also, even if you do use a list (and I would!), remember that you can also follow students' lead, and the words that emerge in your reading curriculum, to investigate morphemes that come up in your read-aloud text, or that children express curiosity about. I've found it's less important the order that you teach affixes or roots, and more important that you foster a sense of word consciousness and an understanding of how these word parts affect meaning.

The fabulous, and perhaps unexpected, thing about teaching morphology is that children adore it. They love deciphering the parts of words. They love the gestures that are part of kinesthetic learning. They love coming up with related words. They love how a little knowledge lets them see connections and meanings. I've taught and observed these lessons with teachers in classrooms full of multilingual learners, in classrooms full of highly proficient readers, and in classrooms where children are not yet reading a lot. Every time, children catch on quickly and get fired up to share words that begin with **in** or end in **able** and so on. I find that you'll often get more effective transfer when learners can follow up on a morphology lesson with an invitation to notice similar words in the books they are reading. Children jot, with great excitement, words from their independent reading or book clubs to add to morphology charts. Since one of the whole points of teaching vocabulary is to increase students' comprehension when they are reading independently, it seems like a good idea to orchestrate opportunities for learners to transfer and apply their vocabulary knowledge to their reading.

In terms of pedagogy for teaching morphology, the lessons that follow blend ideas from Orton Gillingham (Pajor, 2023), from Tim Shanahan (2018), and from the authors of *Shifting the Balance* (2023). This is not a precise breakdown, but from *Shifting the Balance* you'll recognize the notion of deliberate, planned morphology instruction, with a multimodal approach; from Orton Gillingham the particularly kinesthetic learning theories of say it, write it/trace it in your hand, act it out; from Shanahan the emphasis on noticing words in texts and of playing with word creation. You should add your own spin with your students. They will suggest gestures to demonstrate morpheme meanings. They will create visuals, they will offer extensions. The main tips I would give is to keep these lessons relatively short and focused, to send children off with encouragement to apply what they've learned as they read and write, and to invite learners to bring new words to the class's attention.

One quick note about morphology vocabulary! *Affixes* are any morpheme that, when attached to a word or root, changes its meaning. Affixes include *prefixes* and *suffixes*. In some languages, they also include *infixes*, which are inserted in the middle of a word. *Roots* are the core, most basic part of a word that carries meaning. For example, in the word **happiness**, the root word is **happy**. Roots can't always stand alone as a word—for example, in the word **reject**, the root is **ject**. In this chapter, you'll teach prefixes, suffixes, and roots. You may see references to *bases* in morphology as well. A base can include a root, or a root with an affix, and it stands alone as a word. For example, you can add the prefix **un** and the suffix **ness** to the base word **happy**.

I haven't found it necessary to teach the terms for subsets of morpheme types such as free, bound, derivational, inflectional. At the same time, I've seen plenty of elementary teachers who prefer to teach children these terms and use them often in class. If you do want to teach children about morpheme types, I think the two most practical to refer to include:

free morphemes—can stand alone as words. Examples: **happy, dog, book**.

bound morphemes—cannot function alone as words. Examples: **un, ing, dict**.

In terms of supplies and tools, you'll find it tremendously helpful to dedicate a part of your classroom wall to visibly charting the morphology explorations that emerge from your instruction and children's inquiry. You'll find that you and your students return to them again and again, adding new words, combining prefixes and suffixes to new roots, and generally becoming word sleuths. You may want to encourage students to keep word study notebooks, or linguist journals, because you'll find they organically return to their morphology studies as they read.

Many teachers document their morphology instruction using a Morphology Wall

It's also very helpful for multilingual learners if, during the inquiry sessions, when students are collecting and sharing words they know that to include a morpheme you are teaching, you provide a "bank" of some familiar choices which they can combine into words, which they can then share with the class.

Multilingual learners may lean on a small bank of familiar prefixes to add to the new root they learn. This small scaffold sets them up to be successful during the class inquiry.

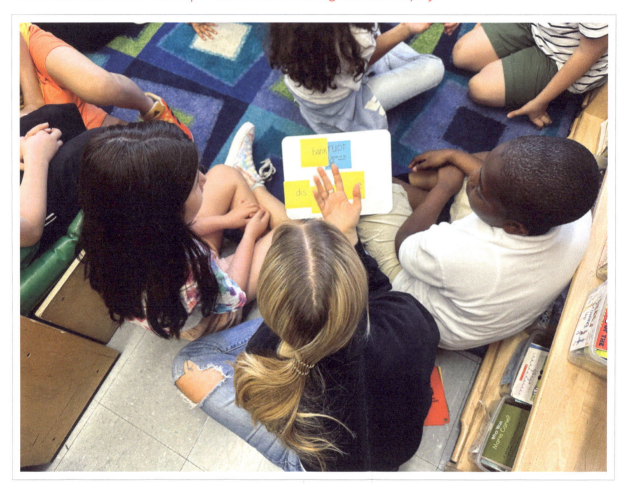

Learning Goals

Expect your learners to become wildly curious and increasingly alert to how words work. Expect their expertise to increase as they absorb Latin and Greek affixes and roots. Expect them to notice similarities and differences across languages. Expect to see effects in their spelling!

Here are some specific learning goals that are built into this work:

- To deepen students' knowledge of common prefixes and suffixes.

- To deepen students' knowledge of common Latin and Greek roots.

- To increase students' alertness to new words in what they are reading.

- To widen the repertoire of skills readers bring to figuring out the likely meaning of new words.

Text Recommendations

Unlike the vocabulary collecting and application of Chapter 1 and Chapter 2, the lessons in this chapter will begin with direct instruction. You'll teach children the meaning of a morpheme and engage them in applying that knowledge. It isn't critical that you have a read-aloud text to anchor this work. That said, it you may still find it helpful to have a familiar text nearby, where you can show children examples of how increased word consciousness leads you to notice more about the vocabulary in what you are reading—and lets you figure out likely meanings of words. For example, you can return to the first page of *Evelyn Rey Is Moving Away*, where Daniela says "everything has **disappeared**"—an opportunity to notice morphology. There are dozens of words that include prefixes and suffixes. The main goal here is to demonstrate how word consciousness changes what you notice as you read.

Opportunities for Transfer and Application

The two places where your learners should transfer and apply their knowledge immediately will be in their writing work and their independent/club reading. As writers, your learners will become more expert and flexible word creators and have more understanding of why words are often spelled the way they are. They'll also be able to do more with verb tenses, as they become more confident with suffixes such as **ed, ing, s**, and so on. This same knowledge of suffixes that show verb tense helps readers track simultaneity and sequence. Is the character talk**ing** with a friend while walk**ing** to the store, or had they talk**ed** with the friend before walk**ing** to the store? You might continue to explore in shared reading or interactive writing how suffixes help readers and writers track and control time. As well as collecting charts to represent each morpheme, you may want to display an anchor chart to remind students of their burgeoning morphological knowledge.

An anchor chart helps learners remember and transfer skills and habits

Studying morphology intersects especially well with:

- spelling strategies while writing

- writing in any genre

- verb tenses in narrative writing

- noticing and figuring out new vocabulary in any text

- test prep

- intervention groups

- enrichment groups

Assessment Options

There are formal and informal ways to assess children's knowledge of morphology—and more important, how they apply this knowledge. You'll notice, below, that I have not listed "give a quiz on the meaning of ten prefixes." I think often about how Freddy Hiebert suggests privileging usage and application over memorization (2011, 2020). The overall goal of these lessons is to increase children's curiosity about words and to increase their specific knowledge of common prefixes, suffixes, and roots, not so they have memorized the word part, but so they are more flexible word solvers. Celebrate when they bring a new word to the class's attention. Create word charts to capture investigations. Invite students to collect words related to your morphology instruction. Some possibilities for assessment include:

- *Word charts*. Invite children to create their own—or shared—word charts, where they jot words that include the prefix, suffix, or root you are teaching. They might post these in the room or keep them in a word study notebook.

- *Sticky Notes While Reading*. Invite children to be extra alert to works in the books they are reading that include the prefix, suffix, or root you are teaching. They can collect these and add them to your class chart.

- *Peer Instruction*. Have students prepare a micro-lesson on a prefix, suffix, or root, to teach to another student or group.

- *Word Study Notebooks or Linguists Journals*. Have students keep a notebook, with a page dedicated to each morpheme inquiry. They can add new words as they come across them in their reading. They can also jot non-examples, as they come across them in their investigations.

Links to Standards

Reading Anchor Standard 4: Interpret words and phrases as they are used in a text, including determining technical, connotative, and figurative meanings, and analyze how specific word choices shape meaning or tone.

Language Anchor Standard 4: Determine or clarify the meaning of unknown and multiple-meaning words and phrases by using context clues, analyzing meaningful word parts, and consulting general and specialized reference materials, as appropriate.

Language Anchor Standard 5: Demonstrate understanding of figurative language, word relationships, and nuances in word meanings.

Lesson 4.1

Magical Morphemes

Considerations

Lesson summary: In this session you will introduce/review the role of *morphemes*—the smallest parts of words that carry meaning. You'll explain what morphemes are and give some examples while inviting learners to divide some words into morphemes. You don't need to go into detail about free and bound (though you can!), but you will introduce the terms **prefixes, suffixes,** and **roots**. You'll also introduce the terms **morphology** and revisit **etymology** and **word consciousness**.

This work helps ground the morphology explorations you'll be diving into in academic language, so your learners, too, will be able to talk about the parts of words.

Estimated lesson time: 10 minutes.

Materials and preparation: You'll need to display word consciousness vocabulary, and you'll display a few words that you'll break down into morphemes on a chart.

Additional lesson options: Morphemes are present in every language. You might invite your multilingual learners to explore morphemes in more than one language, so that they build their knowledge of language structures. Often students will see parallels and begin to recognize patterns.

Launching the Lesson

Invite students to share their understandings of some vocabulary-related word consciousness. Then explain what morphology is and what morphemes are.

You might say, "Linguists, you are definitely becoming **word conscious**! That means you're curious about and alert to how words work. I'm going to show you some vocabulary related to word consciousness. Some you'll know, and some you probably won't. Talk with your partner—what words here have we talked about?"

To explain morphology, you might say, "A new word here is **morphology**. **Morphology** is the study of the parts of words, especially how words are made up of **morphemes**. A

morpheme is the smallest unit of meaning in a word. Like the word **dog** is a single morpheme, because you can't break it into smaller parts. But the word **backyard** has two morphemes."

Engagement—Investigation and Collection

Demonstrate separating a word into morphemes, explaining prefixes and suffixes as you do so, and invite kids to take some words apart into morphemes.

For example, you might say, "Let's try this work out, linguists. Let's take the word **read**. This word only has one morpheme—you can't break it into smaller meaning groups. But the word **reread** has two morphemes. **Read**, and **re,** which is a **prefix**, a morpheme that usually means 'again,' as in … read again! You'll learn a lot more about **prefixes** and **suffixes** soon. For now, a **prefix** is a morpheme at the start of the word, and a **suffix** is a morpheme at the end of a word. Both change the meaning of a word. For instance, if we add the suffix **ion** to **act**, we get **action**. When we see trouble, we rush into **action**!"

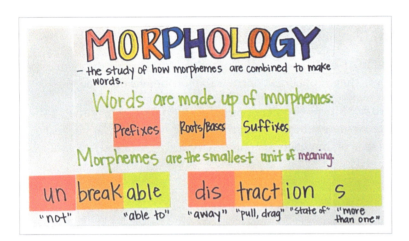

Invite kids to try. "Try breaking these words into morphemes! How many parts, or morphemes, are there in **unkind**, **walked**, and **disagreement**? What are some other words that might have two, three, or four morphemes in them?"

Application

Invite learners to think and talk about how knowing more morphemes and becoming more word conscious might help them figure out new words.

You might say, "Linguists, I bet you're thinking already how, when you know the meaning of some of these morphemes, you'll be able to figure out the meaning of more words! Yes! As you get to know morphemes, you'll be able to figure out lots of new words!"

The work students will create during and after the lesson might look like ...

¡Morfología!

Morpheme practice

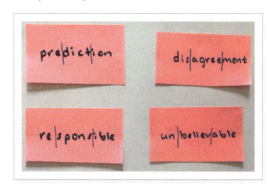

Starting with Prefixes

Considerations

Lesson summary: In this session and in the series you'll explore around prefixes, you'll introduce the concept of prefixes, and teach students the meaning of one in each session. This lesson demonstrates the prefix **un**, which means **not**. You can, and should, replicate this lesson, each time teaching a new prefix that is on your list or that has come to your class's attention.

Steps for teaching prefixes include:

- teach the meaning of the prefix—acting it out, explaining it, jotting it

- share some examples of words with this prefix—explaining and jotting

- engage children in writing the prefix "in their hands"/on whiteboards

- engage children in acting out its meaning with a gesture

- invite children to share and explain words they know that include this prefix

- collect these words

- send children off, suggesting they continue to collect words as they read and/or be alert to words with this prefix

This work initiates a protocol for studying prefixes, suffixes, and roots or bases. It develops children's curiosity and awareness of word parts and supports readers in figuring out the meanings of words, using their knowledge of prefixes, and writers in creating more words.

Visit the website www.vocabularyconnections.org to download a protocol for teaching morphology.

Estimated lesson time: 8 minutes.

Materials and preparation: You'll need to write the prefix, its meaning, and a collection of related words on a chart that you can display. Some students, especially multilingual learners, will benefit from a small starter collection of a few roots they can easily create words from. You can simply jot these on sticky notes and post them to a small whiteboard so children can form a few words.

Additional lesson options: In this lesson, you teach **un**, one of the easiest prefixes. You'll want to repeat this lesson for a series of 8–10 prefixes per grade, such as **re, pre, non**, and so on. I suggest following the sequence recommended by Cunningham,

Burkins, and Yates (2023), in their "Multi-year Plan for Systematic Morphology Instruction," which they offer free to teachers as a downloadable accompaniment to *Shifting the Balance 3–5* at TheSixShifts.com. If your grade is the first to teach morphology, then begin with the easiest list, and look at your calendar to think about how many prefixes and suffixes you might teach in one year.

If you are teaching multilingual learners, use an AI partner to research what prefix matches **un** in their languages. For example, Spanish tends to use **in, im**, and **ir** to mean **not (increíble, imposible, irresponsable)**. Ukrainian uses the prefix **не** (неможливо, недружній, нецікаво—**impossible, unfriendly, uninteresting**).

Launching the Lesson

Introduce the concept of prefixes and teach the meaning of the prefix un, making an action for not as you define it. Share a few words that include this prefix, and explain their meanings, jotting the prefix, it's meaning, and the words so children can easily see as well as hear the meaning.

For example, you might say, jotting as you explain, "We've talked about **prefixes**, but let's review. A **prefix** is a **morpheme**. It comes at the start of the word and affects the meaning of the word. Today's prefix is **un**. It means **not**." (Make a motion with your hand as if forbidding something, with a stern face, or invite students to come up with a gesture.) "Some words that include **un** are **unreadable**, like when I rush and my handwriting is **unreadable**—you cannot read it. Or **unstable**—this desk rocks, it is **unstable**—not stable. Or my computer is **unplugged**—it's not plugged in. Once you understand that **un** means **not**, you can figure out a lot of vocabulary words that include this **prefix**."

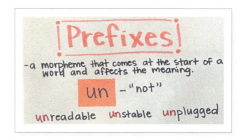

Engagement – Investigation and Collection

Invite learners to join you in writing the prefix and acting it out. Then invite children to share and explain some of the words they know that have this prefix. Collect these words. Sometimes you need to explain a word that does start with un but it isn't a prefix, like unite, or unicorn.

You might say, "Join me in learning this prefix. First, let's write the prefix three times." (Children can write it in their hands using their "magic notebooks" or on whiteboards.) "Now let's act it out. To show NOT, let's put our hands out, like we're saying NO! Let's do that three times, saying not and acting it out!"

Then engage students in sharing words they know. "I bet you know some words that begin with **un**. Talk to your partner—if you have a word, explain what it means and give an example! I'll collect some of your examples on our chart."

If you bump into a non-prefix word, like **unite**, simply say, "Oh, that's what we call a *non-example*. It does start with **un**, but it doesn't mean **not**. Let's write those words over here, on the side, and we can investigate them later!" (Most of the words in which **un** is not a prefix are based on the Latin morpheme **uni**, meaning **one**, such as **unicycle, unique**, and so on.)

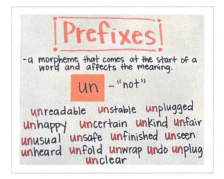

Application

Send children off, encouraging them to be alert for more words that include this prefix. Suggest that they try to figure out the meaning of these words, using their knowledge of this prefix.

You might say, "As you're reading today, linguists, be extra alert to words that include this prefix. You might jot them on a sticky note, and then you can add them to our word collection. And most importantly, pause to figure out their meaning, now that you are an expert with this prefix!"

The work students will create during and after the lesson might look like ...

Keeping track of prefixes

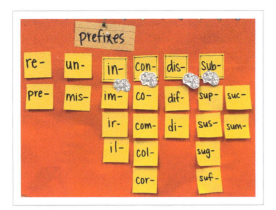

Prefijos que significan no o sin

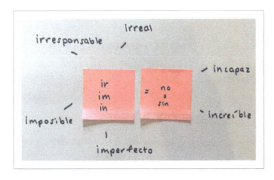

Exploring the prefix **mis**

Onward with Suffixes

Considerations

Lesson summary: In this session and in the series you'll do around suffixes, you'll introduce the concept of suffixes, and teach students the meaning of one in each session. This lesson teaches the suffix **ful**, which means **full of** or **characterized by**. You can, and should, replicate this lesson each time teaching a new suffix that is on your list or that has come to your class's attention.

Steps for teaching suffixes include:

- teach the meaning of the suffix—acting it out, explaining it, jotting it

- share some examples of words with this suffix—explaining and jotting

- engage children in writing the suffix "in their hands"/on whiteboards

- engage children in acting out the meaning with a gesture

- invite children to share and explain words they know that include this suffix

- collect these words—and notice if any have prefixes children have already learned

- send children off, suggesting they continue to collect words as they read and/or be alert to words with this suffix

Visit the website www.vocabularyconnections.org to download a protocol for teaching morphology.

This work builds on the protocol for studying prefixes, deepening learners' knowledge of morphology. As students learn to use their knowledge of prefixes and suffixes, they become more expert word solvers and word creators. They'll also become more word conscious overall, confident that they understand how words work and can approximate the meaning of many words.

Estimated lesson time: 8 minutes.

Materials and preparation: You'll need to write the suffix, its meaning, and a collection of related words on a chart that you can display. As when learning prefixes, some students, especially multilingual learners, will benefit from a small starter collection with a couple of roots that they can create words from. You can simply jot these on sticky notes and post them to a small whiteboard so children can form a few words.

Additional lesson options: In this lesson, you teach **ful**, one of the easier suffixes. You'll want to repeat this lesson for a series of 8–10 suffixes per grade, such as **or, er,**

ly, etc. Again, I suggest following the sequence recommended by Cunningham Burkins, and Yates (2023), in their "Multi-year Plan for Systematic Morphology Instruction," which they offer free to teachers as a downloadable accompaniment to *Shifting the Balance 3–5* at TheSixShifts.com. If your grade is the first to teach morphology, then begin with the easiest list, and look at your calendar to think about how many prefixes and suffixes you might teach in one year.

If you are teaching multilingual learners, use an AI partner to research what suffix matches **ful** in their languages. For example, Spanish tends to use **oso (amoroso, poderoso, respetuoso)** or **al (profesional, personal)**. Comparing linguistic systems helps students become more flexible with language.

Launching the Lesson

Introduce the concept of suffixes and teach the meaning of the suffix ful, making an action for ful as you define it. Share a few words that include this suffix and explain their meaning. Jot the suffix, its meaning, and the words so children can easily see as well as hear the meaning.

For example, you might say, jotting as you explain, "You've learned several **prefixes**, and today we'll move to **suffixes**. A **suffix** is also a **morpheme**, only it comes at the end of the word. Today's suffix is **ful**. It means **full of**. Let's come up with a motion for this suffix together. Show your partner your ideas, use your hands! How about … we cup our hands together, to show that someone is full of this? Some words that include **ful** are **joyful**. When I am filled with joy, I am **joyful**. Or **truthful**—when your words are full of truth you are **truthful**. You'll be able to create a lot of words, and figure out words as you read, when you understand this suffix."

Engagement—Investigation and Collection

Invite learners to join you in writing the suffix and acting it out. Then invite children to share and explain some of the words they know that have this suffix. Collect these words. If they suggest words that also have familiar prefixes, call attention to how much they know.

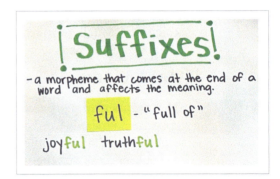

You might say, "Join me in learning this suffix. First, let's write the suffix three times." (They can write it in their hands or on whiteboards.) "Now let's act it out. To show **ful**, let's hold our hands like we are holding a bowl full of something **wonderful**!"

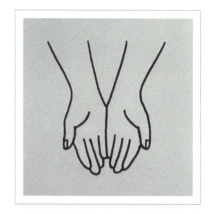

Then engage students in sharing words they know. "I bet you know some words that end with **ful**. Talk to your partner—if you have a word, explain what it means, give an example! I'll collect some of your examples on our chart."

If children suggest words that also have a familiar prefix, celebrate how much they know. For example, "I love the way you are using your prefix knowledge, with words like **disrespectful** and **unhelpful**! Tell your partner, in **disrespectful** what does the prefix mean, and how do the prefix and suffix shape the meaning of this word?"

Application

Remind children that as they read, they can be alert for more words that include this suffix—and words that also include prefixes they know. Suggest that they try to figure out the meaning of these words, using their knowledge of word parts.

You might say, "As you're reading today, linguists, be extra alert to words that include this suffix. You might jot them on a sticky note, and then you can add them to our word collection. And most importantly, pause to figure out their meaning, now that you are an expert with this suffix! And be extra, extra alert to words that include this suffix and include prefixes you know—then you can really use all your tools to figure out the word."

The work students will create during and after the lesson might look like ...

As children add suffixes they can also use their prefixes

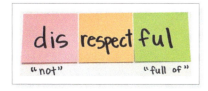

Sorting out how **s** and **es** can be suffixes on nouns as well as verbs

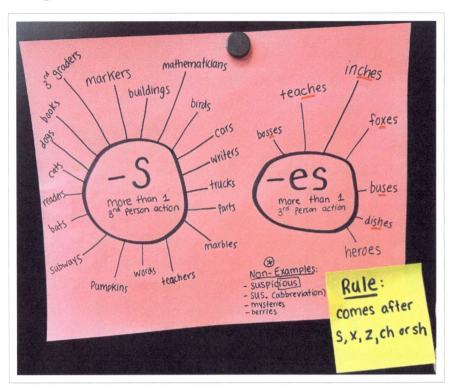

Keeping track of suffixes

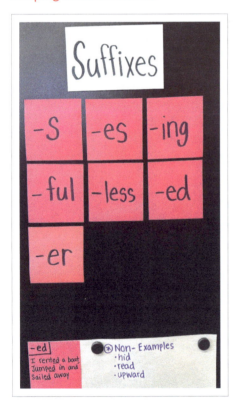

Keeping track of non-examples for further exploration

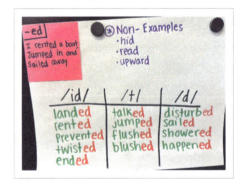

Special Suffixes Control Time

Considerations

Lesson summary: In this session you'll call students' attention to a particular set of suffixes—the verb tense endings **s, es, ed, ing**. Ideally, you've already taught each of these as part of your sequence of suffixes, and here you review them with a new focus on how they are used to show time. You'll invite students to join you in an inquiry, noticing how these suffixes help readers understand *when* something is happening in a story— they help writers show their readers about timing. Together, you'll investigate verb endings in a snippet of a story.

This work helps students as readers and writers. For readers, it raises students' alertness to verb tense, and increases their understanding of how verb endings change the sense of when an action takes place. For writers, it deepens their knowledge of how to control verb tenses in order to control timing.

Estimated lesson time: 10 minutes.

Materials and preparation: You'll need a small chart with suffixes that are also verb endings, and a snippet of a story with these suffixes. You'll hand out copies of this story excerpt to students.

Visit the website www.vocabularyconnections.org to download a story excerpt.

Additional lesson options: In this lesson, you'll demonstrate with a narrative example. You might follow up with an expository example. For instance, students might investigate how the suffixes, the verb tenses, in claims, create different meanings, such as:

Lying to my mother *causes* a lot of trouble in my life.

When I lied to my mother, it *caused* a lot of trouble in my life.

Doris *wanted* a dog mostly because she was so lonely.

Doris *wants* a dog because she is so very lonely.

You can also investigate similar suffixes in Spanish or other languages with your multilingual students, such as **ando** for **ing** in Spanish—**hablando, andando, llorando**.

Launching the Lesson

Review the suffixes which are also verb endings, and their meanings.

You might show a small chart, and remind students, "Let's take a moment to review the suffixes you learned that are also verb endings. Look at this chart, and with your partner, say the suffix, trace it in your hand, act it out, and explain its meaning. Tell each other some other words that include it! Use them in some sentences."

s, es	present tense	Someone does this all the time.	walks explores vanishes	Sarah walks to school every day at 8 a.m.
ed	past tense	Someone did this in the past.	walked explored vanished	Sarah walked to school at 7 am at her old school.
ing	present participle	Happening right now!	walking exploring vanishing	Sarah is walking to school right now.

Engagement—Investigation and Collection

Invite students to join you in investigating the different suffixes attached to verbs in a snippet of a story. Have them pair up and act out the scene, and then invite them to try to explain how these suffixes affect meaning.

You might say, "Let's investigate how writers use these suffixes to show *when* something is happening. I'm going to hand you a snippet of a story. With your partner, try three things. One, underline the verbs—the action words, like walk and talk. Two, circle the suffixes on these verbs—the verb endings. Three, act out the story! One of you be Sarah and one of you be Juan. Then four, try to explain to each other how these suffixes, these verb endings, are meaningful—how does the writer use them to show timing—when something is happening?"

Sarah walked slowly down the dark street. She sensed movement behind her. Slowly she reached for her phone, and called Juan, her best friend.

"Juan, I'm walking down the street. Some creature is following me. I can hear it creeping. It sounds like it's walking on four legs. And I can hear it breathing—it's snuffling and wheezing! I'm two blocks from your house."

"I'm coming right now!" Juan yelled into the phone. He ended the call and dashed out the door. He wanted to get to Sarah as fast as possible.

You might summarize, saying, "I heard you say that the **ed** suffix is past tense, and it shows that at some point before the story started, Sarah walked down the street and called her friend. It makes the action seem sort of calm. But then when it's **ing**, and it's happening right now, it gets very exciting. Something is following Sarah, **creeping** and **snuffling** and **wheezing**!"

Application

Encourage students to consider their verb endings as special suffixes, that help them show action as writers, and interpret actions as readers.

You might say, "Linguists, when you are writing, use the knowledge you have of these special suffixes, these verb endings, to control when things are happening. And when you are reading, pay attention, be alert to how these suffixes are clues to timing in the story you are reading."

The work students will create during and after the lesson might look like ...

Exploring suffixes as meaningful indicators of verb tense and action

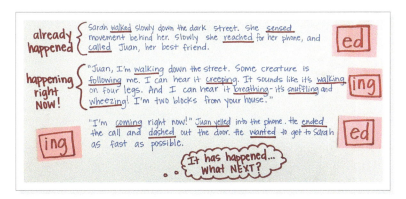

Revisiting a read aloud text through the lens of verb tense, suffixes, and time changes

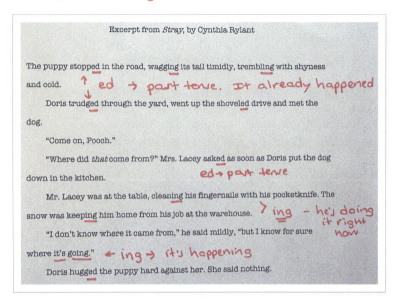

Documenting suffixes that are important verb endings to indicate tense

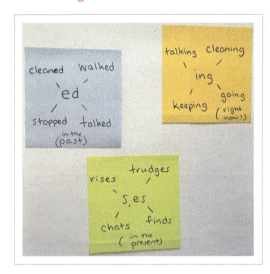

Getting to Know Roots

Considerations

Lesson summary: In this session you'll teach students about roots, and you'll give them an opportunity to decipher the meaning of words using their knowledge of prefixes and suffixes along with a new root. You'll teach one specific root in this session—**port**, which means "to carry." You can, and should, replicate this lesson, each time teaching a new root that is on your list or that has come to your class's attention.

This work adds to students' linguistic flexibility, increasing their ability to figure out the meanings of words as they read, using their knowledge of prefixes, suffixes, and roots. It also adds to their powers as writers and spellers, as they become more confident word creators.

Estimated lesson time: 10 minutes.

Materials and preparation: You'll need to write the root, its meaning, and a collection of related words on a chart that you can display. As when you taught prefixes and suffixes, some students, especially multilingual learners, will benefit from a small list of familiar prefixes and suffixes that they can attach to **port** to create new words from. You can simply jot these on sticky notes and stick them to a small whiteboard so children can form a few words.

Additional lesson options: In this lesson, you teach **port**, one of the easier roots. You'll want to repeat this lesson for a series of 8–10 roots, such as **aud, dict, rupt**, etc. As with prefixes and suffixes, I suggest following the sequence recommended by Cunningham Burkins, and Yates, in their "Multi-year Plan for Systematic Morphology Instruction," which they offer free to teachers as a downloadable accompaniment to *Shifting the Balance 3–5* at TheSixShifts.com.

If you are teaching multilingual learners, especially ones who speak Romance languages, you can share words in those languages that share the root you are teaching. For instance, in Spanish, **transportar, portador**, and in French, **déporter, portable**, include the same root.

Launching the Lesson

Introduce the concept of roots and teach the meaning of the root port (to carry), making an action for port as you define it, or asking learners to come up with an action. Share a few words that include this root, and explain their meaning,

jotting the root, its meaning, and the words so children can easily see as well as hear the meaning.

For example, you might say, jotting as you explain, "You've learned a lot of prefixes and suffixes, and you've become so word conscious! Today we'll begin our exploration of roots. If you think of a tree, the root is what gives it strength. It's the same in words—the root carries the central meaning. You can learn roots just like you learned prefixes and suffixes, and you'll be able to figure out and create so many words!"

Then define **port**. "We'll start with the root **port**. It means to carry. What action should we use—maybe holding our arms, like we are carrying books, or something?"

Engagement—Investigation and Collection

Invite learners to join you in writing the root and acting it out. Then invite children to share and explain some of the words they know that have this suffix. Collect these words. If they suggest words that also have familiar prefixes, call attention to how much they know.

Children will be familiar by now with this protocol, so you can give lean instructions. "Let's say it, write it, and act it out, three times. Then let's collect and share some words!"

!Roots!
- carries the central meaning of a word.

port - "to carry"

import report portable
transport passport
transportation support
seaport airport teleport

Application

Remind children that they can use their knowledge of roots to figure out tricky vocabulary as they read, and to create words as they write.

You might say, "You are becoming so expert, linguists. Remember, you can use this knowledge to figure out tricky words as you read, and to create new words as you write. Be extra alert today to words that include this root—see if you can figure out the meaning of the word with your super word consciousness powers!"

The work students will create during and after the lesson might look like ...

Collecting words with the root **rupt**

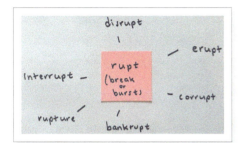

This "bank" of common prefixes supports multilingual learners in suggesting new words that include the root **rupt**

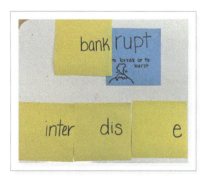

Exploración de la "port"

Word Builders

Considerations

Lesson summary: In this session you'll teach learners that they can use all their knowledge of prefixes and suffixes and roots to create words. This session will work best if you've taught several prefixes and suffixes so that students can apply their knowledge as word builders. You'll do a quick demonstration, and then engage students in partnerships to create words and to do their best to explain their probable meaning to each other. Note—if you are teaching third graders, and aren't venturing into roots extensively, this is still worth exploring so they get practice creating words with prefixes and suffixes—simply provide two or three roots for them to practice with and explain their meaning.

This work increases students' linguistic flexibility. It increases their confidence as word builders, and it deepens their consciousness of how words work, and how they can figure out meanings using parts of words. Students can approximate the meaning of hundreds of words with this knowledge, as writers and readers.

Estimated lesson time: 10 minutes.

Materials and preparation: You can teach this lesson with no supplies, and simply lean on your morphology wall/collection as a resource for children. Or you can provide cards with prefixes and suffixes and roots (usually printed in different colors), for children to combine. Providing cards gives more support and will definitely help your multilingual learners.

Visit the website www.vocabularyconnections.org to download morpheme cards.

Additional lesson options: In this session, some students may create a few words whose meanings they don't know—in fact, they may not even be sure if they are words. A good follow-up inquiry is for students to look these words up with their partner, to learn their meanings. You can set students up with SchoolAI, which will teach them etymologies as well as meanings. For your multilingual learners, creating words using morphemes in all their languages will increase their linguistic competencies and cognitive flexibility.

Launching the Lesson

Demonstrate word creation, using a few familiar prefixes and suffixes with a familiar root, such as **spect**, which means to **see** or **observe**.

You might say, "Linguists, you've learned many prefixes and suffixes, and some roots as well. You know how to figure out the meaning of many tricky vocabulary words, using your word consciousness. Well, you can also create words with this knowledge! For instance, watch me create some words with these morphemes—these prefixes, suffixes, and roots—and see if you come up with ideas as well. If you do, whisper them to your partner! Let's get started with the root **spect**, which means to see or observe."

 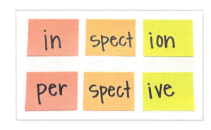

Engagement—Investigation and Collection

Set partnerships up with an envelope or baggie with morpheme cards and invite them to create words together. Encourage them to explain the words' likely meanings as well, and to keep track of words they are unsure of.

You might say, "Partners, you each have an envelope with cards in it—prefixes and suffixes, as well as a few roots. See how many words you can create! If you're unsure of the meaning of one of these morphemes, these word parts, ask another partnership, or turn to our morphology wall."

Application

Encourage students to carry their word consciousness with them, as readers and writers, and to use all their knowledge to figure out word meanings and create new words. Also encourage them to be alert to new morphemes, and to notice similarities across languages.

You might say, "Linguists! Your word consciousness will be a superpower! Think of all you know about morphemes—word parts! You can use this knowledge to figure out word meanings, and to create new words. Even more importantly, you'll be alert to new word parts, and you can learn their meanings so that you'll be able to figure out hundreds of vocabulary words, in English and in other languages!"

The work students will create during and after the lesson might look like …

Jotting morphemes to create new words

Using morpheme cards to create words

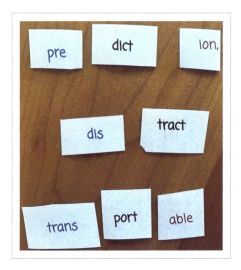

An anchor chart helps learners remember and transfer skills and habits

Part
III

Domain Vocabulary

Collecting Domain Vocabulary

The Scope of These Lessons— What's Going to Happen!

In these lessons, you'll motivate your students to collect and discuss domain vocabulary—words that are important in topics they are studying. Their domain vocabulary collections will function as a kind of lean note-taking process. This work will be most powerful when it is linked to content studies or any nonfiction study in reading or writing that involves research. Maybe your students are studying the water cycle, or the solar system, or civil rights. Whenever students learn new content, part of their learning should be domain vocabulary. Capturing domain vocabulary is a way to hold onto knowledge, to speak with expertise, to practice technical explanations, and to increase comprehension of complex texts (Pearson et al., 2020). You can repeat and solidify these lessons whenever students are learning new content, so they come to expect collecting, sorting, talking about, and applying new vocabulary as work they do whenever they study something new.

Trust that students will, indeed, notice domain terms that feel important, whether they are learning from a nature video or a book. They will start with a couple, and they may be unsure of their meaning. As they continue to research, they collect more words, and they clarify meaning. Children are curious, intelligent beings who will naturally pick up vocabulary that feels important as they learn about a topic. They will notice highlighted words and they'll listen for new explanations. They are eager to learn and new vocabulary is part of new learning.

With these lessons, you'll give your students systems to collect vocabulary, and it's remarkable how many words they'll begin to assemble and investigate. There are two aspects that are most important to this work—*context* and *usage*. Link children's vocabulary collections to the context of their studies and create lots of opportunities for usage.

In the next chapter, we'll dive into context clues. Here, make sure your learners have accessible text sets, and trust that texts will teach students many new words and concepts, whether they are watching a science video or reading a trade book. In *Teaching Words and How They Work*, Hiebert reminds us that "texts are a primary source for gaining new vocabulary" (Hiebert, 2020, ch 1). Duke, Ward, and Pearson (2021) also demonstrate the ways that texts support readers in building content knowledge, and they remind teachers that students can bring their knowledge of morphology, compound words, context clues, and related content to their reading.

Ideally, as you teach these lessons, students are engaged in a content study. Whether they are studying the solar system or flag football or the pros and cons of solar versus wind energy, there will be domain vocabulary related to the content. The vocabulary emerges as students move from one text to another, from one learning experience to the next. For instance, if students are studying endangered animals and human impact, and they begin with the manatee, they'll first learn terms like **sea cow, flippers, whiskers, flukes**. As they keep learning, they'll learn **mammal, nurse, pollution, entanglement,** and **sea grass**. All content studies mirror this path, introducing many new terms that students begin to focus on and sort out as they learn more. In content studies, children will learn an extraordinary number of Tier 2 and Tier 3 words *as* they read books and articles, watch informational videos, listen to scientists and historians, take notes, and talk and write about what they are learning. In no time you'll hear students speaking with remarkably expert vocabulary—especially when you can combine reading and writing curriculum so learners are gathering vocabulary as they research, and explaining it as they write and present.

Sketching and labeling as a way to gather vocabulary and build knowledge

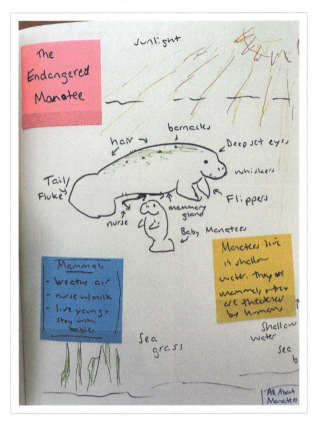

It helps students come to this work with a sense of power when you affirm and amplify the expert vocabulary they already know, as well as the ways they learned this vocabulary. Some of your learners are experts in baseball or soccer. Some know a tremendous amount about dinosaurs. Some know about horses, or ballet, or chess, or the Dominican Republic, or cooking that is important in their family and culture. Your classroom is full of experts who know Tier 2 and Tier 3 words in many languages. You'll start this work, therefore, by giving them an opportunity to share their vocabulary expertise, their passions, their funds of knowledge, and their linguistic capital within your learning community. You can return to what you learn about your students—across your teaching. In *Not This but That: No More Teaching Without Positive Relationships* (2020), Howard, Milner-McCall, and Howard suggest that we, as teachers, need to research and expand students' cultural and linguistic capital, and also their aspirational capital. As we find out more about children's passions, we not only know them better, we learn more about how they learn, and can amplify those funds of knowledge.

There are a few things you'll want to understand about domain vocabulary and how it resonates in a classroom. One is that a lot of domain vocabulary words are *concepts*. **Photosynthesis**, for example, is a process. When a child explains photosynthesis, they are explaining a scientific process. So collecting domain vocabulary, sorting it and explaining it often is a way for learners to understand a topic deeply. Second, it helps to collect words that are important in a topic, not just *hard* words. When a child explains why **shallow water** is important to manatees, they are explaining one reason that manatees are endangered. Including words whose significance is contextual encourages nuanced, contextual explanations.

Perhaps most importantly, some vocabulary words are concepts that are complicated and deeply referential and merit discussion as well as care for individual students. **Segregation**, for example, is not a vocabulary word you would simply pre-teach with a definition. It's a concept that carries within it histories of racism and suffering. You'd want to read and watch texts and talk about histories past and present. You'd want to study examples. You'd want to think about the students in front of you, especially students of color who may feel generational trauma related to this system. You'd be respectful that the word itself brings oppressive histories into the classroom. In *Antiracist Reading Revolution: A Framework for Teaching Beyond Representation Toward Liberation* (2024), Sonja Cherry-Paul encourages us to bring our full humanity to our teaching, and to strive to create identity-affirming classroom spaces. This includes thinking about how some studies can be painful. Sara Ahmed, author of *Being the Change: Lessons and Strategies to Teach Social Comprehension* (2018), warns us that each child and family will encounter the curriculum differently. One child may encounter the word **drought**, and have distressing experience with it, while for another it may be an abstract, rarefied concept.

Finally, as you set out to teach domain vocabulary collection intentionally, think about the different modalities students can employ, as well as the many opportunities you can foster for students to explain these vocabulary terms to each other and to audiences outside of the classroom. Because it helps if students can sort their vocabulary often, in multiple ways, you might give them envelopes and cards, which they can tuck into their notebooks or folders. Some students might prefer a digital collection. The main thing is that you want to make it easy for students to sort and rearrange their words. They might pull them out and explain the significance of terms to each other. They might lay them out to use in a presentation or a piece of writing. They might practice conceptual sorts, arranging them in categories. They might use these words as they predict today's weather, or explain what is happening outside the classroom windows. Each time they explain a term, they deepen their content knowledge and make it more likely they'll remember the vocabulary.

Learning Goals

Expect your learners to take on an astounding depth and breadth of domain vocabulary. When students engage in deep content studies, they often become proficient not only with precise Tier 2 vocabulary but also with specialized Tier 3 vocabulary. Expect your students to engage often in explanations and comparisons. This is a recursive process, by which they first collect vocabulary and practice initial explanations, and as they learn more, they broaden their collections and deepen their knowledge. Expect learners to use this vocabulary in their presentations and their writing, and to apply their knowledge while reading fresh texts.

Here are some specific learning goals that are built into this work:

- To deepen students' knowledge of domain vocabulary related to content studies.

- To deepen students' knowledge of contextual meanings of vocabulary terms.

- To introduce ways to collect vocabulary, including sketching and labeling and conceptual vocabulary sorts, as a way to hold onto knowledge.

- To introduce semantic mapping as a method for synthesis and analysis.

- To widen the repertoire of skills readers bring to sorting, explaining, and applying domain vocabulary in context.

Text Recommendations

For students to acquire domain vocabulary, they need to learn from a wide variety of compelling, accessible texts. They will be able to move up levels of complexity as they become familiar with vocabulary and content. A great text set, then, offers multiple levels, multiple modalities, and multiple perspectives. If you are launching science or social studies content, for example, you might start with nature and science videos, so students will hear new vocabulary, including pronunciations, and see visual explanations and examples. When children have a wide range of multimodal texts, learning from print and digital sources, they'll absorb a tremendous range of domain vocabulary as part of building knowledge. As students learn vocabulary from an easier text on a topic, they can apply that vocabulary to help them read the next, slightly more challenging text. It's a fabulous, reciprocal linguistic relationship.

In the next chapter, we'll dive deeply into context clues. For that, I use excerpts from Marta Magellan's beautiful and significant book, *Up, Up and Away, Monarch Butterflies* (2024), illustrated by Mauro Magellan, with photographs by James Gersing. In this chapter, therefore, each teacher demonstration also continues a focus on Monarchs and butterflies. You can, of course, substitute bees, or sea turtles, or the water cycle, or civil rights, or soccer, or any content of your choice. Every content has its own specialized vocabulary.

The most essential structure for this work is that children are researching a topic. They can be in research clubs (my favorite), partnerships, or an all-class study. This can include an extended study that lasts weeks, or one in which students shift topics every few days, or it can be a micro study. What's wonderful about teaching students *how* to acquire domain vocabulary, as opposed to teaching them individual vocabulary words, is that they can apply the strategies you teach to all the content they study and to every inquiry process they engage in.

In these lessons, students need a place to jot and collect vocabulary in a variety of ways. This might be a field notebook—these are great for science topics—or a researcher's notebook, or a reader's notebook. They'll sketch and label. They'll add captions to these sketches. They'll also collect vocabulary with cards, which they usually keep in envelopes. You could do this digitally, but overall, the analog version lets children easily take out their vocabulary and sort it in different ways, lay it out to use in their writing, move it around to prepare for a presentation, and so on. I often get gift envelopes, which are colorful and inexpensive in bulk, but any envelope that researchers can tuck into their notebooks or folders will do.

Opportunities for Transfer and Application

Your learners will become adept at both noticing and collecting significant, conceptual vocabulary that arises in the texts they study, and considering terms that are contextually important to their topic. They'll develop systems for collecting vocabulary, they'll practice conceptual sorts, and they'll learn to *use* this vocabulary through repeated oral practice. Try to capitalize on these growing powers by finding opportunities for your learners to transfer and apply these skills. If you start this work in a science study, transfer it to social studies. If children begin by studying endangered animals, help them see that even as the content changes, the skill set of how to research, how to learn not just new vocabulary but all the knowledge that comes with understanding and being able to explain the significance of that vocabulary, stays the same.

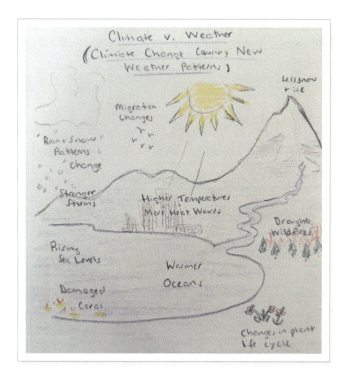

When students are encouraged and coached to sketch and label, collect vocabulary, and use expert words in their note taking across all their content studies, they become both fluent and flexible with these important skills. You might create an anchor chart to remind students of these habits.

An anchor chart helps learner remember and transfer skills and habits

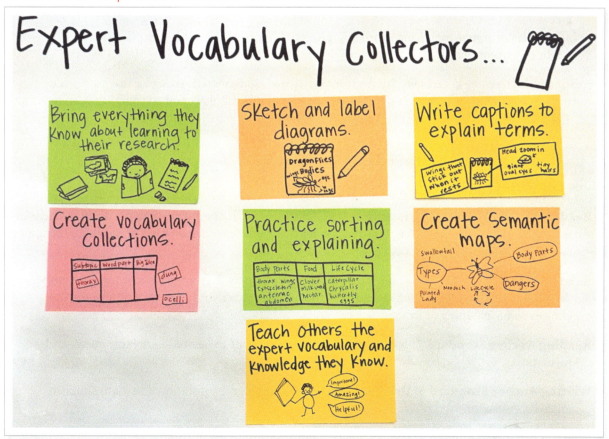

Deepening students' independence with collecting conceptual vocabulary increases their capacity for lean note taking, explaining context and connections, and speaking and writing with expert language. This work will fit beautifully with:

- Nonfiction reading

- Research-based information writing

- Research-based argument writing

- Content studies

Assessment Options

You should see an increase in the depth and nuance of students' understanding of domain vocabulary and concepts, as well as the expertise with which they speak and write about topics.

Some possibilities for assessment (including self-assessment) include:

- *Vocabulary sorts.* Invite students to sort their vocabulary collections and to explain their categorization system, as well as why each word they included is significant in this study.

- *Preparation for research conversations.* Listen to or record partner or research club conversation, noting how students use their expert vocabulary to talk about content and build ideas.

- *Semantic mapping.* Ask students to create a semantic map with some of their vocabulary, one that shows relationships, connections, cause and effect, or sequence.

- *Information or argument writing.* Note how students not only include but explain domain vocabulary in context.

- *Student-led teaching discussions.* Invite students to use all their tools to lead a teaching discussion of their topic, in which they teach peers or families expert vocabulary and content knowledge.

Links to Standards

Reading Anchor Standard 1: Read closely to determine what the text says explicitly/implicitly and make logical inferences from it; cite specific textual evidence when writing or speaking to support conclusions drawn from the text.

Reading Anchor Standard 4: Interpret words and phrases as they are used in a text, including determining technical, connotative, and figurative meanings, and analyze how specific word choices shape meaning or tone.

Reading Anchor Standard 7: Integrate and evaluate content presented in diverse media and formats.

Writing Anchor Standard 5: Draw evidence from literary or informational texts to support analysis, reflection, and research.

Writing Anchor Standard 7: Gather relevant information from multiple sources.

Speaking and Listening Anchor Standard 1: Prepare for and participate effectively in a range of conversations and collaborations with diverse partners.

Speaking and Listening Anchor Standard 6: Adapt speech to a variety of contexts and communicative tasks, demonstrating command of academic English when indicated or appropriate.

Language Anchor Standard 5: Demonstrate understanding of figurative language, word relationships and nuances in word meanings.

Language Anchor Standard 6: Acquire and accurately use general academic and content-specific words and phrases sufficient for reading, writing, speaking, and listening; demonstrate independence in gathering and applying vocabulary knowledge when considering a word or phrase important to comprehension or expression.

5.1

Experts Explain

Considerations

Lesson summary: In this session you'll launch students into a content study of your choice, by first positioning them as expert learners, and finding out more about what they're already passionate about. You'll invite students to share topics and content they know a lot about (from baseball to WWII airplanes), and to teach others some of the special vocabulary of that topic, as well as to share how they learned that vocabulary and knowledge.

This work affirms students' identities as knowledge builders, learners who already know a lot about how to study a topic they care about, and who already have a lot of expert vocabulary. It also allows you to refer to specific students' expertise, and to foster learning alliances.

Estimated lesson time: 10–15 minutes.

Materials and preparation: You won't need anything special for this session, though it is lovely to collect students' interests and expertise on a chart in the room, with their names, so that you can refer to it in many circumstances.

Additional lesson options: If you teach informational writing, you can build on this work by inviting students to imagine how an information article or book would go, that taught others about their topic. Even if you then move into a class research topic, students will have a better understanding of structure, and more confidence, when they've practiced with a topic they know well and love.

Launching the Lesson

Let students know that you'll be diving into a content study, where they'll become better researchers, and learn a lot about new topics, including a lot of new vocabulary. Suggest to students that they already know a lot about how to do this work, because they have things that they love and study on their own. Share an example from your own childhood, including some of the expert terms you knew.

You might say, "We're about to dive into a study of Monarch butterflies. You'll be naturalists, and entomologists, and we'll all teach each other along the way, so we know more about how to protect these beautiful creatures who can't speak up for themselves. Along the way, you'll learn a lot about research, and a lot about collecting expert vocabulary. But before we start, I bet you already have topics you know a lot about, that you've been fascinated by for years. For instance, when I was a kid, I was fascinated by horses. I knew the difference between **Thoroughbreds, Clydesdales** and **Arabians**." (Whatever your topic is, share some expert vocab, maybe show some images.) "We couldn't afford an actual horse, but I knew the different types of horses, because I read novels and nonfiction, I watched videos and films, I visited stables when I could, I talked to horse people."

Get out your old notebooks if you have them, to share childhood passions

Clydesdale

Arabian

Engagement—Investigation and Collection

Invite students to share with a partner something they are fascinated by, and to teach that partner some of the expert vocabulary of that topic. Give a few possible examples, and then suggest they start by jotting a few expert words on sticky notes.

To launch partnership conversations, you might say, "I know you have things you know a lot about too. For some of you it might be soccer, or baseball, for others it might be a book series, or maybe you're fascinated by an animal, or by a period in history, or by a kind of cooking. Think for a moment, and when you have an idea, jot a few of the important, expert vocabulary terms you know from that topic on sticky notes. Like, if you're thinking of baseball, you might jot **third base** or **inning** or **fielder**. When both of you have jotted a few words, share your topic with your partner. Tell them what you love about this topic, and teach them a few expert vocabulary words."

You can also capitalize on students' independent learning habits, by saying, "Take another minute, and tell your partner *how* you learned all this vocabulary, and all about this topic. I'll listen in and capture some of what you say in a chart."

Application

Suggest that whenever learners set out to study something new, they can lean on what they already know how to do—how to immerse themselves in a topic, learn from every possible source, and along the way acquire and use lots of expert vocabulary.

Harness children's agency as a bridge to the topic you're studying. You might say, "You know so much about how to learn, how to research something, and along the way, how to learn a lot of expert vocabulary. You'll use what you already know about learning from every possible source, and do that same work of becoming expert, gathering up expert vocabulary, as we embark on this study of endangered creatures."

The work students will create during and after the lesson might look like ...

One research club shares their passions

Students share their learning methodologies that they already are good at!

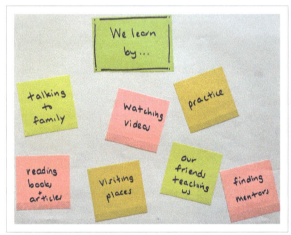

This young baseball specialist shares his expert vocabulary digitally

Vocabulario futbolístico

Lesson 5.2

Sketching and Labeling

Considerations

Lesson summary: In this session you'll teach students that one of the simplest and most effective ways to begin to collect expert vocabulary (and gather information) about a nonfiction topic is to sketch and label diagrams. You'll first share a couple of examples of labeled sketches from famous thinkers' notebooks. Then you'll demonstrate this work by starting a diagram of a butterfly, with a label for one body part, and you'll invite students to practice by watching a brief nature video and sketching and labeling more of the parts of a butterfly.

This work supports your students with one of the most essential forms of note taking and vocabulary collection. For scientists and social scientists, annotated diagrams are a critical form of note taking. Becoming fluent with this skill will support your students as note-takers and researchers.

Estimated lesson time: 10 minutes.

Materials and preparation: You can access a small collection of famous notebook pages that feature annotated diagrams, as well as sketches of the monarch butterfly, on the website www.vocabularyconnections.org.

You'll also show a brief nature video on butterflies (or the content of your choice) so students can practice sketching and labeling. Video-based research is more effective for launching this work than showing a diagram in a book, because it promotes synthesizing rather than simply copying.

Additional lesson options: First, try to extend this lesson by giving students time to continue researching, sketching, and labeling. As your students learn to sketch and label as a form of note taking and vocabulary collection during content studies, you can also teach them to leave white space for additional notes, to color-code their diagrams, and to return to their sketches to add annotations. These skills will serve your students in all of their content studies.

For your multilingual learners, encourage them to learn terms across languages, so that they are building up academic, domain vocabulary in all their languages.

Another good follow-up lesson is to teach students to add to their diagrams as they find new information, rather than simply copying ones they find in books, or starting a new diagram each time they learn something new.

Launching the Lesson

Rally students to the simplicity and efficiency of sketching and labeling as a tool for note taking and vocabulary collection. Show some examples of famous thinkers' notebooks, and invite students to notice some of their characteristics.

You might say, "Researchers, one of the most efficient ways to take notes and to collect vocabulary is to sketch and label. Scientists call these annotated diagrams. Let's take a look at a notebook page from a famous naturalist. Her name is Jane Goodall. What do you notice about her notes?"

Engagement—Investigation and Collection

Demonstrate how you might get started, by watching a video and starting an annotated diagram (a simple sketch with a few labels). Then engage students in trying this work out by sketching their own diagrams and adding more labels. Finally, ask them to use their diagrams to explain to each other what they know about the scientific parts of butterflies.

You might say, "Let's try this work out. Let's watch a snippet of a nature video about butterflies. Let's try to sketch a diagram, and label it as we learn some important terms ... hmm, it feels like we've learned they have wings, let's try to sketch those ... And researchers, sometimes the word might not be new—like we know that birds have wings. But the wings of butterflies are shaped differently than birds' wings, and when you explain this to a partner, you can use your diagram and your label."

Continue with, "Now let's watch a bit more, and see if we can add any more labels. Listen for any scientific terms, or vocabulary that might be important when talking about butterflies." After watching, sketching, labeling, add, "Use your diagram and your labels to explain to each other the important, scientific parts of butterflies. What do they use each part for?"

Application

Encourage students to continue this work as they research, as a way of note taking and capturing important vocabulary, and also of synthesizing. Also encourage them to use these labeled diagrams as a way of teaching others, practicing explanations with expert vocabulary.

You might say, "Researchers, this note-taking strategy works with any content, not just butterflies. If you are in the sea turtle group, you won't label wings you'll label ... flippers. Go find out, and be ready to teach the rest of us! Remember, anytime you are researching something new, sketching and labeling is a way to hold onto new information and important vocabulary. I'll give you one tip—you don't need to start a new diagram every time you learn something new. Often, you can add to your existing diagram, so that it becomes a way of synthesizing, or pulling together information from different sources."

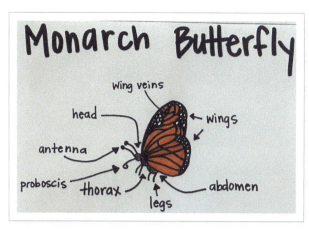

The work students will create during and after the lesson might look like ...

This young entomologist labels the parts of a bee with domain vocabulary

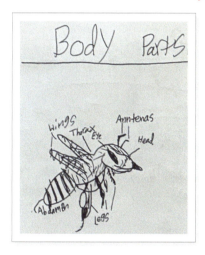

Sketching and labeling science topics

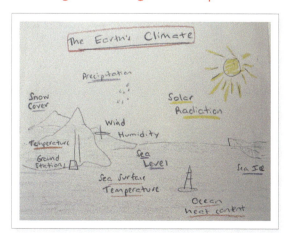

This young researcher collects scientific words for the parts of a Monarch

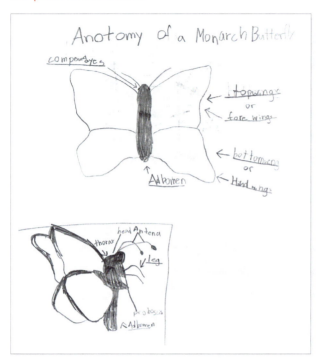

Lesson 5.3

From Labels to Captions

Considerations

Lesson summary: In this session you'll extend sketching and labeling. You'll teach students that they can deepen and share their knowledge by turning their labels into captions. You'll start by having students explain one of the labels from their diagram from Lesson 5.2. Then you'll suggest that a caption can teach that same explanation. You'll also suggest that turning a label into a caption may require a return to the research process, to find out more about that term.

This work will increase students' usage—they'll return to the vocabulary they've been collecting, and explain it, first orally and then in writing. It's always useful for learners to practice scientific and historical explanations. They'll not only deepen their comprehension and retention of domain vocabulary, they'll expand their knowledge of the content they are studying, and their confidence in themselves as burgeoning experts.

Estimated lesson time: 10 minutes.

Materials and preparation: You'll need the annotated diagram you started in Lesson 5.2 of a Monarch. Today you'll add to that diagram by turning one or two labels into captions. Your students will also need the diagrams they started yesterday. For practice, your students will also need the diagrams they started in Lesson 5.2. If you followed Lesson 5.2 with more research time, students might decide to return to other diagrams they sketched and labeled during that extension.

Additional lesson options: As with Lesson 5.2, your students will become more proficient if they have opportunities to apply this work by doing more research. You might demonstrate how you can return to a diagram and add new captions as you learn information from new sources. For more advanced researchers, you can also show how you can add sources/references inside of a caption. Finally, you might introduce a whole new lesson on teaching kids how to return to research when they find it challenging to explain one of their labels/write a caption. Sometimes they've heard the word and written it down, but they don't yet fully grasp its meaning or significance. Learning to go back and clarify when terms are unclear will support students in becoming independent.

If you are teaching information writing, you can make a clear parallel by teaching a revision/elaboration strategy of turning labels into captions in the articles, books, and reports students are writing.

Launching the Lesson

Invite your young researchers to share the diagrams they sketched and labeled in (or after) Lesson 5.2. Have them practice explaining one of the labels.

You might say, "Naturalists! Expert linguists! Take out the diagram you made yesterday, where you sketched and labeled to capture important information and vocabulary ... now try to explain one of your labels to a partner. Tell why it matters, its importance. Like, 'Butterflies need wings in order to ...' or 'A butterfly's wings work by ...'"

Engagement—Investigation and Collection

Suggest that just as they gave explanations out loud, your young linguists can also write these explanations as captions as a way to deepen and share their expert knowledge. Show how you do this work, and invite them to write one caption and share with their partner.

You might say, "Researchers, linguists! You have learned some expert vocabulary! I heard you explaining how butterflies use wings to migrate! You are really sounding like scientists. I want to give you a tip. As you start to know more, you can deepen and share this knowledge by turning some of your labels into captions. For instance, I'll try to capture what we said about the proboscis, by jotting a caption ... then you try it, with one of your labels."

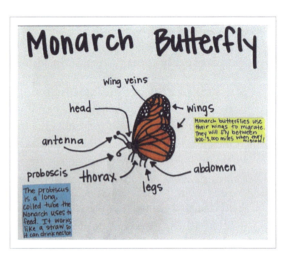

Application

Encourage students to apply this strategy to all their note taking and writing, with any content or area of study. Also remind them that if they find it challenging to draft a caption, that might be a sign that they need to do a bit of research to find out more about it.

You might say, "Researchers, you can do this work whenever you are researching, taking notes, or writing. Say more! Don't just say a word, explain it. Often, it's the explanation that is fascinating. I'll also give you one tip. If it's hard for us to explain the word, that often means that, even though we've seen it or heard it, we need to research to find out more to really understand its significance."

The work students will create during and after the lesson might look like ...

Adding captions as sticky notes to extend a labeled sketch

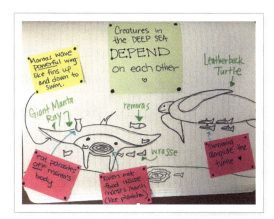

This young entomologist adds a caption to her sketch and labels

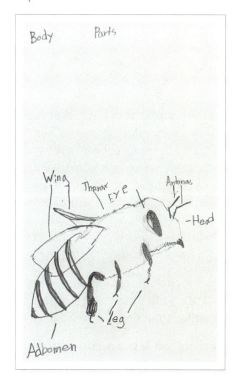

Adding captions to social studies sketches

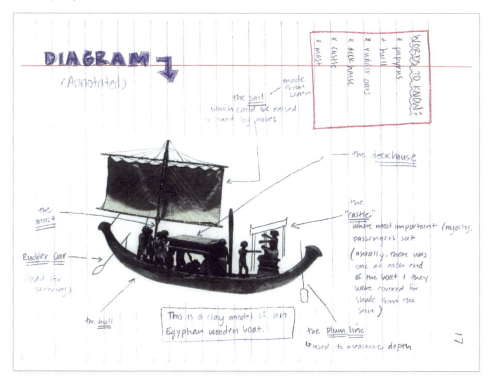

Collections and Sorts

Considerations

Lesson summary: In this session you'll teach students a different way to collect domain vocabulary that is similar to the work they did with literary vocabulary. That is, they can create collections, which they can then sort in a variety of ways. With each sort, students explain why they think the word is important in the context. One tip—focus on words that are important to the focus topic, not only new hard words. **Wings**, for instance, are important to Monarch butterflies. **Wings** is not a new, hard word, but talking about its significance in context will be as important as talking about the **proboscis**. And wings are important to migrating Monarchs in a way that is different from hawks or penguins, for example.

This work with conceptual vocabulary sorts gives students a lot of oral language practice—increased usage. It helps them see connections, to practice explanations, and to understand domain vocabulary as concepts. It's also a precursor to semantic mapping.

Estimated lesson time: 10 minutes.

Materials and preparation:
You'll need some note cards or words on large sticky notes that you can display and move around, or a digital system (not a typed glossary, but any system that allows students to move words around into different groups easily). Your learners will need the same materials. It helps to have a system that is easily accessed. Greeting card envelopes and note cards work well. In the lesson, you'll hand out envelopes and note cards, with a small starter set of words. Visit the website www.vocabularyconnections.org to download Monarch butterfly word cards.

Additional lesson options: It can be powerful to do a gallery walk as clubs create different sorting methods. Some may sort chronologically, others by category, and so on. Inviting research clubs to explain their sorts gives them another opportunity to articulate their thinking and use content-specific vocabulary. Your multilingual learners may write the words in more than one language, on different sides of their cards.

It's also very helpful for writers to get out their collection and do some sorting before they write, asking, "What words do I need to define for my readers?" and "What terms will I use in the first part of my writing, and in the next part?"

Launching the Lesson

Suggest to students that another way to gather domain vocabulary that allows researchers to collect a lot of words, and to use them in different ways, is to start a sortable collection. Show an example of a small collection you've started that includes words related to butterflies, and invite students to add words as well, emphasizing collecting words that are important to this topic.

You might say, "Researchers, linguists! As you start to learn more about a topic, another way to collect vocabulary is to start a collection that will allow you to gather many words, and sort and use them in different ways. To do this, you ask yourself: What words/terms are important to this topic?

"Then you jot these, each one separately. If you are researching with a partner or club, you can each jot some words, then see how you overlap, and decide how their words might help you build a bigger collection. For instance, here are some words that feel important to Monarch butterflies."

Engagement—Investigation and Collection

Invite students to add words to this collection. Then engage them in practicing some different ways to sort.

You might say, "I'm handing your partnership an envelope with these words and some blank cards. Tell your partner, what are some other words we could add? Jot those on cards!"

Then model sorting them, saying, "Now let's try some sorting. And as you sort, you might add more words! Let's see, maybe we could sort by categories—like we could do words for things butterflies eat, and words for things that eat them … or we could sort by words we know well and can explain to each other, and ones we want to learn more about … or we could even do categories like what they eat, where they live, life cycle …"

Give a tip. "Every time you sort a word into a specific group, explain why you think that word should be included! Then you can try a different sort, explaining which words go together and why."

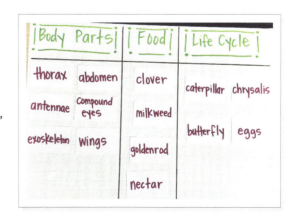

Application

Encourage learners to create their own word collections whenever they are learning new content and to practice sorting them in preparation for conversations and for writing. Also suggest that research clubs can use this method as a way to anchor expert content conversations.

You might say, "Researchers, don't wait for someone to start a collection for you from now on. Whenever you are researching, you can start a word collection, yourself or with a partner or club. And you can use this method of sorting and explaining as a way to talk about what you're learning or rehearse for presentations and writing."

The work students will create during and after the lesson might look like ...

Sorting climate and weather vocabulary

Translated vocabulary collection

Vocabulary cards can include important information

Two-sided vocabulary cards with sketches on one side
to support learners with complex vocabulary

Semantic Mapping

Considerations

Lesson summary: In this session you'll build on the conceptual vocabulary sorts students practiced in Lesson 5.4. You'll move students beyond sorting words into categories, to making semantic maps—a way of showing the relationship between words. For instance, a semantic map might show the life cycle of the Monarch butterfly with each vocabulary word, and its placement, marking a particular phase of this cycle. Or a semantic map could show the placement of offensive strategies and players for a particular play. Semantic mapping can include flow charts and timelines that show sequence. They can also have layers—there could be a life cycle in the center, with habitats and predators flowing into appropriate parts of that cycle. You'll demonstrate semantic mapping with Monarch butterflies, laying out the vocabulary collection from Lesson 5.4, and inviting students to imagine and contribute to a shared semantic map.

This work helps learners clarify relationships, categories, and processes. They'll often map cause-and-effect relationships, or parts of a topic, or a sequence of events in a process. Semantic mapping encourages learners to synthesize and analyze information. The visual elements activate engagement, retention, and understanding.

Estimated lesson time: 10 minutes.

Materials and preparation: You'll need the word collection from Lesson 5.4, and you'll create (or show) a semantic map for butterflies. Visit the website www. vocabularyconnections.org to download sample word collections and a semantic map for the Monarch butterfly.

Additional lesson options: In the lesson, your learners will practice with Monarch butterflies. If they are engaged in a different content study with their research clubs, they might go on to create semantic maps on that topic too. Often students prefer larger paper, so they can add to this map across their studies. Another follow-up is to take each term on a concept map and show learners how to add sketches and captions, so the map becomes a rich synthesis tool and peer-teaching tool.

Launching the Lesson

Remind students of the different ways they practiced sorting their expert vocabulary, inviting them to get out their vocabulary collections and practice one quick sort. Then introduce the notion of semantic maps as a way to show overall relationships.

You might begin, "You've been collecting and sorting vocabulary. Get out your expert vocabulary collection, and with a partner, sort some of your words. Explain why you put words in different categories, based on your research."

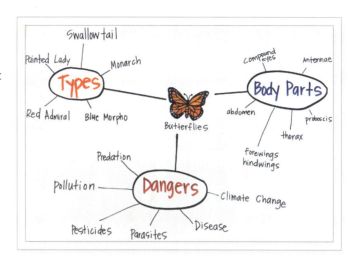

To introduce semantic maps, you might say, "There is another, even more sophisticated way to sort and display your vocabulary. It's called *semantic mapping*, and it means choosing some terms, and creating a map as a visual to show the relationship between these terms. Semantic maps often show cause and effect, or sequence, or main topic and subtopics. They always show complex relationships. For example …"

Engagement—Investigation and Collection

Invite students to join you in drafting a semantic map for Monarch butterflies.

You might say, "Let's try some of this work together. Semantic maps are really good, we know, for sequence, or cause and effect. So, let's start with the life cycle of the monarch. First, we'll think about the vocabulary we know, and try to map it …"

You may decide to extend the work, saying, "Now let's see if we can add layers. For instance, we could add some of the dangers during the butterflies' life cycle."

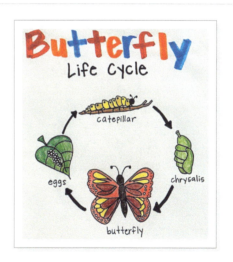

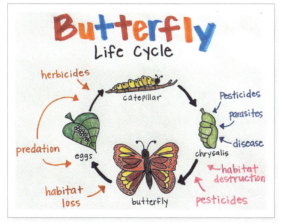

Application

Encourage learners to create semantic maps as a way to capture, synthesize, and share what they learn, and to deepen their understanding of the relationship between expert terms.

You might say, "Researchers, you can create semantic maps in articles and books you write, as a tool for a presentation, and as a way for a research team to share their learning. Semantic maps will deepen your understanding of expert terms, and it will help you synthesize and analyze complicated relationships."

The work students will create during and after the lesson might look like …

Semantic maps in science are often flow charts

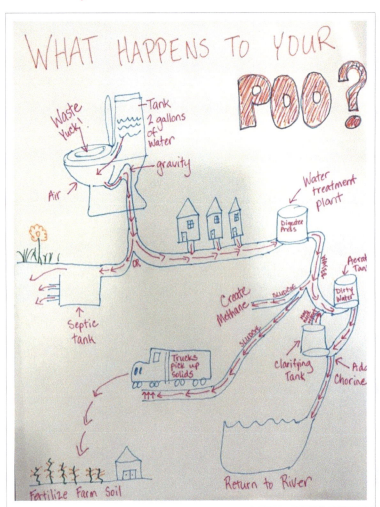

Semantic maps in social studies are often timelines

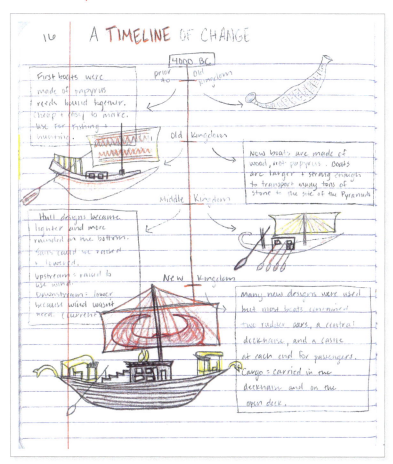

Mapping the vocabulary and relationships of segregation

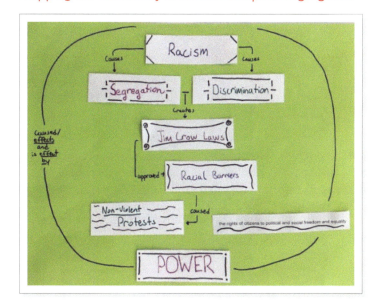

Lesson 5.6

Cross-Content Conversations

Considerations

Lesson summary: In this session you'll show your learners how to use their collections to launch cross-content conversations. Each partnership or research club will gather their annotated diagrams, their vocabulary collections, and their semantic maps. They'll use these to rehearse what they might teach a different partnership or club. Then they'll have cross-content conversations, using their expert vocabulary tools to teach each other.

Estimated lesson time: 15 minutes.

Materials and preparation: You will need your labeled diagram, your sample vocabulary collection, and your sample semantic map. Your students will need all their vocabulary notes, tools, and collections.

Visit the website www.vocabularyconnections.org to download sample diagrams, word cards, and semantic maps.

Additional lesson options: These kinds of conversations are also a beautiful way to wrap up and celebrate a research unit. Children can meet with family groups, teaching them about their content, sharing their sketches and their maps, engaging them in sorting and explaining vocabulary. It is also expert rehearsal for presentations and for writing, giving students opportunities to use domain vocabulary as a way of explaining knowledge.

Launching the Lesson

Rally students to celebrate and share their learning by teaching others. Show them how to use their diagrams, their collections, and their maps, as tools to rehearse and engage in expert conversations. Demonstrate with your own sample tools.

You might say, "Researchers! You know so much expert vocabulary—you know so much knowledge about your topic! Today, I want to show you how to use all your tools—your diagrams, your collections, and your maps—as a way to rehearse expert conversations and teach others. For example, I'm thinking that I want to share with my family everything we've learned about Monarch butterflies. I want us to plant milkweed. I want us to keep track of when Monarchs are migrating. I want us to see what we can do to help protect these magical creatures. So … maybe I'll start with my diagram, and I'll teach my family how amazing these creatures are. Then maybe I'll move to my map, to show them how migration matters to their life cycle. Then maybe I'll let them try sorting some of the vocabulary, to get them interested in learning more."

172

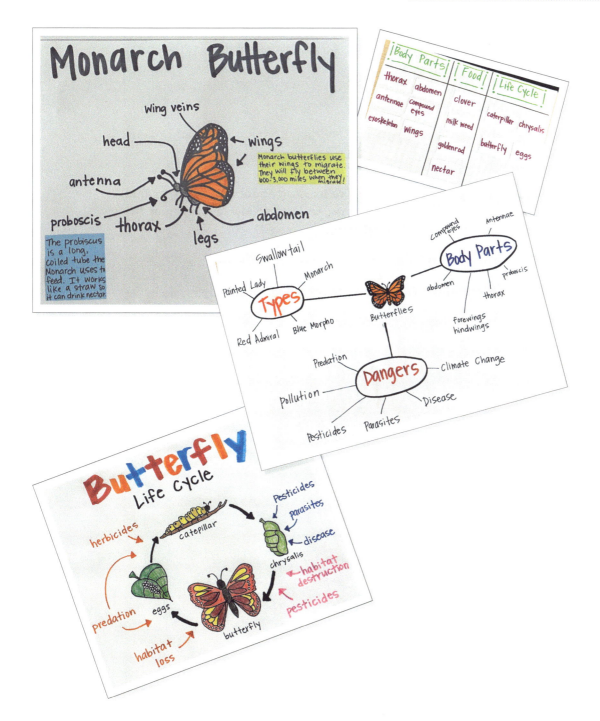

Engagement—Investigation and Collection

Invite students to gather their materials and rehearse their conversations. Then set them up to teach a different partnership or club (or families). Give a tip that as expert linguists, they know a lot of vocabulary that they should explain!

You might say, "Researchers, you can do this work too! Gather your tools. Use them to rehearse what you'll teach another group. Figure out how you can make the conversation interactive. Can your listeners add to your vocabulary collection? Or try sorting? Could they ask questions about your map? Also, I want to give you one tip. You are expert linguists now! You know so many specialized vocabulary words about your topic. Remember that you'll need to explain these in your conversations with people who aren't as familiar with them!"

Application

Encourage students to apply everything they've learned about collecting expert vocabulary whenever they study something new, and to add these strategies to their note-taking skills as well.

You might say, "Researchers, you not only know a lot of expert vocabulary, you also know a lot about how to collect expert vocabulary, by sketching and labeling, writing captions, creating vocabulary collections, sorting vocabulary, and making semantic maps. Use these skills whenever you are studying something new, or teaching others!"

The work students will create during and after the lesson might look like ...

Sketches, labels, semantic map, captions all in one!

An anchor chart helps learner remember and transfer skills and habits

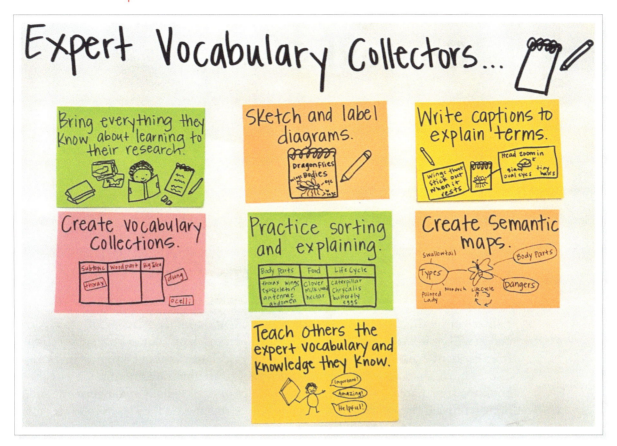

Diving into Context Clues

The Scope of These Lessons— What's Going to Happen!

The lessons in this chapter aim to increase students' competencies—both as readers and as writers—with context clues. Young readers pick up a lot of vocabulary simply from incidental learning, especially when they read deeply about a topic. For example, as they move from a nature video on manatees to an illustrated nonfiction picture book about manatees, to more complex articles or books about endangerment and human impact, they learn a huge amount of vocabulary. As they learn to make smart, strategic text choices, they'll learn vocabulary from more accessible texts, and apply that knowledge to read more challenging texts in the same topic. In the midst of this natural, incidental learning, your readers are processing a lot of context clues, which is why they pick up so much vocabulary—and why deep reading builds so much knowledge.

This type of incidental learning, though, is most effective for students who have access to a lot of texts, and who can read those texts with deep comprehension. It's also important to teach them to recognize and decipher context clues, so that all your readers become adept at accessing more challenging texts. One way that nonfiction becomes more complex is that writers will use a variety of context clues to explain or illustrate domain vocabulary—and a lot of that vocabulary will be scientific or historical concepts that are complicated.

In his blogpost for *Reading Rockets*, entitled "How I Teach Students to Use Context in Vocabulary Learning," Tim Shanahan explains his theory of "passive scaffolding," which he describes as guiding students to determine meaning from the text (2023). The emphasis, then, is not on pre-teaching individual words, but instead, on teaching children methods for figuring out the meaning of words. Passive scaffolding emphasizes transferable strategies. Otherwise, Shanahan warns, "most reading programs tend to include a handful of context exercises and then undermine those lessons with how they guide reading the rest of the year." The overall goal is always reading comprehension.

In the lessons that follow, you'll teach your students a variety of ways that authors tend to provide context for domain vocabulary. You'll teach them to investigate embedded definitions, complicated text features, examples that act as illustrations of a concept, and above all, context. Learning to recognize these techniques, to investigate meaning, to lean on a repertoire of strategies, will build your students' competencies as readers. It will also extend their skills as writers, especially if you return to these competencies in information writing and argument writing. Anytime they are writing nonfiction, suggest that your learners consider the expertise level of their audience, and make thoughtful decisions about how they will explain expert vocabulary and complex concepts. Building a reciprocal relationship between reading and writing context clues will deepen and expand your students' linguistic capacities.

You'll go beyond teaching your learners to become adept at context clues. You'll also develop their critical literacies. Vocabulary reflects more than simply expert knowledge. It reflects the author's perspective. It hints at their feelings and stance on the topic. Do they describe manatees, for instance, as **bothersome** for how they entangle fishing nets, or do they describe them as **vulnerable** and **wounded**? The author's word choice creates a *tone*, and that tone will be suggestive of the author's point of view—to the alert and critical reader. In her autobiography, Rosa Parks responded to social studies textbooks continuing to describe her as sitting on a bus because she was **tired** (such as Joy Hakim's textbook, *All the People* (2010), whose original Chapter 15 was still titled: Rosa Parks Was Tired.): "I was not tired physically, or no more tired than I usually was at the end of a working day," states Rosa Parks. She continues, "No, the only tired I was, was tired of giving in" (Parks and Haskins, 1999, 116). Word choice matters.

Learning Goals

Expect your learners to become adept at recognizing and interpreting context clues in a variety of forms. Expect that they will not only decipher more domain vocabulary in the texts they are reading, they will also become more alert readers who understand more literary techniques. Expect their comprehension skills to increase. Expect them to apply this knowledge to their reading and also to their nonfiction writing.

Here are some specific learning goals that are built into this work.

- To deepen students' competencies with contextual clues for domain vocabulary.

- To deepen students' knowledge of domain vocabulary related to content they are studying.

- To build reciprocity between reading and writing, so that your readers bring alertness to literary techniques to their nonfiction reading, and to their nonfiction writing.

- To deepen students' critical literacies, so that they are alert not only to meaning, but also to how word choice suggests authors' tone, stance, and point of view.

Text Recommendations

You can teach these lessons using any texts related to content your class is studying, as long as the text includes a variety of context clues. These lessons in this chapter will return to Marta Magellan's nonfiction book, *Up, Up and Away, Monarch Butterflies*, illustrated by Mauro Magellan, with photographs by James Gersing. Like all of Magellan's books on nature and science, this one is beautiful, it teaches important science, and it uses a variety of nuanced methods to showcase domain vocabulary. You'll see, inside the text, examples of tucked-in definitions, of annotated diagrams, a variety of charts and diagrams, and a glossary. This set of lessons also includes an exploration of accessing vocabulary in nature, science, and history videos, and for that, you'll watch *All About Monarch Butterflies*, a fabulous science video created by the World Wildlife Foundation.

Set your students up to practice this work with text sets that include high-quality print nonfiction, as well as digital texts such as nature and science videos. Print texts offer students quick opportunities to reread, to lay texts next to each other, to move easily from one part of the text to the next. Having the opportunity to read a lot of engaging, compelling print nonfiction on a topic will allow your students to both increase their comprehension and build knowledge. Digital texts such as videos and interactive websites are initially more engaging, but also harder to comprehend. These multimedia texts are great for launching a topic (because they are so engaging), and they are good to return to once learners know more and can access the often rapid presentation of information and vocabulary. Don't shy away from texts that seem more complex, or that don't immediately define every word for learners—it's going to be important for young readers to learn how to navigate these texts, to learn vocabulary *from* texts. As long as they have some accessible texts to help them get started, your students should be able to move at a reasonable pace along a ladder of complexity in the same topic.

Routines and Structures

The most essential structure for this work is that children are participating in ongoing research of a topic. This can be established through research clubs, partnerships, or all-class studies—all of which are preferred over individual learners embarking on a study without a thought partner. Alongside this, the only other essential is that students have access to an engaging text set that offers a variety of vocabulary and content presentation.

Your researchers will need a system for taking notes, including the vocabulary terms and concepts they learn. In the previous chapter, they learned to collect vocabulary terms on cards in an envelope they can tuck into their notebook, and to sketch, label, and caption as a way to hold onto domain vocabulary. If they like, they can continue that system while practicing defining and explaining terms in their writing or you can develop a different note-taking system together.

Opportunities for Transfer and Application

Your learners will become the most adept at navigating complex context clues when they get to practice this work across content studies, and when they apply their learning as readers and writers. That is, children who learn varied methods for deciphering context clues should use those same techniques to explain vocabulary as writers. You might create an anchor chart to remind your learners of the different techniques they've learned for attending to context clues.

An anchor chart helps learners remember and transfer skills and habits

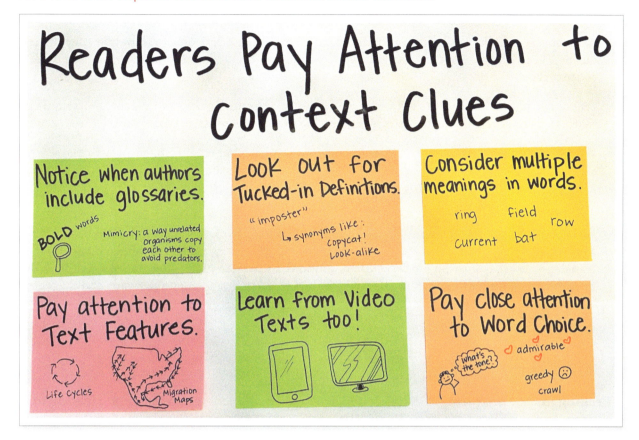

Try to capitalize on the reciprocal relationship of this work, so that students deepen their competencies with context clues as readers and writers. This work will fit beautifully with:

- nonfiction reading

- research-based information writing

- research-based argument writing

- content studies

- test prep

- intervention groups

- enrichment groups

Assessment Options

You should see an increase in the depth and nuance of students' content conversations, and in the specificity and creativity of their writing about content. Assessing what students do as they read is tricky. But pay attention to their strategy application—how students explain vocabulary to each other, how they point out the parts of the text that support their learning, how they use these same tools as writers. Some possibilities for assessment (including self-assessment) include:

- *Annotated texts*. Ask students to annotate a page of text with sticky notes to show how they figured out new vocabulary—what features they used, where they found definitions or examples or other context clues.

- *Peer conferring*. Invite students to teach each other how they are figuring out vocabulary from their texts. Have them use the texts they are researching in their peer instruction.

- *Text-based conversations*. Because we care enormously about comprehension, one way to assess students' control of domain vocabulary is to listen to them talk about what they've learned from a text, what seems most important. Listen for how they use expert vocabulary learned from the text.

- *Nonfiction writing*. Students' writing will demonstrate both their knowledge of domain vocabulary and their awareness of and fluency with writing techniques to explain this vocabulary. Look for transfer—how they incorporate tucked-in definitions and explanations, how they use text features to highlight important terms, how they plan for and teach their audience new words and concepts.

Links to Standards

Reading Anchor Standard 1: Read closely to determine what the text says explicitly/implicitly and make logical inferences from it; cite specific textual evidence when writing or speaking to support conclusions drawn from the text.

Reading Anchor Standard 4: Interpret words and phrases as they are used in a text, including determining technical, connotative, and figurative meanings, and analyze how specific word choices shape meaning or tone.

Reading Anchor Standard 7: Integrate and evaluate content presented in diverse media and formats.

Writing Anchor Standard 5: Draw evidence from literary or informational texts to support analysis, reflection, and research.

Writing Anchor Standard 7: Gather relevant information from multiple sources.

Speaking and Listening Anchor Standard 1: Prepare for and participate effectively in a range of conversations and collaborations with diverse partners.

Speaking and Listening Anchor Standard 6: Adapt speech to a variety of contexts and communicative tasks, demonstrating command of academic English when indicated or appropriate.

Language Anchor Standard 5: Demonstrate understanding of figurative language, word relationships, and nuances in word meanings.

Language Anchor Standard 6: Acquire and accurately use general academic and content-specific words and phrases sufficient for reading, writing, speaking, and listening; demonstrate independence in gathering and applying vocabulary knowledge when considering a word or phrase important to comprehension or expression.

Lesson 6.1 Working with Glossaries

Considerations

Lesson summary: In this session you'll teach students to notice when authors include glossaries, which may be in the form of a list at the end of a chapter or text (or as clickables the reader can access as they read). You'll invite students to practice using both these forms, from a print and online text. One note—as texts become more challenging, the words authors use inside of glossary definitions are themselves harder, and so usually the reader has to move from the glossary to the text and back, and try to explain why this term is important and what that part of the text teaches.

This work will support your students' deftness with using this essential vocabulary tool. Equally importantly, it will support students' reading comprehension and understanding of a topic.

Estimated lesson time: 10 minutes.

Materials and preparation: You'll show an excerpt from *Up, Up and Away, Monarch Butterflies*, written by Marta Magellan with illustrations by Mauro Magellan and photographs by James Gersing (2024). You can easily substitute a different text related to other content that you are studying in class. If so, look for texts that include different forms of glossaries—in the margins, at the end of sections, or in the text.

Additional lesson options: Repeat this lesson with an online article or ebook, such as *Monarch Butterflies*, an online text by National Geographic Kids (2024). Show students how digital authors also highlight vocabulary, and the glossary is in a clickable form. The reader needs to follow the same steps of reading around the word, studying the glossary, and then explaining (or approximating in their explanation) why a term is important to what that part of the text is teaching.

Return to this lesson when students are engaged in nonfiction writing as well! Have them study the nonfiction texts they've read as mentors, looking for how authors include different kinds of glossaries.

Also, be alert to how authors define words, especially in social studies texts. A powerful follow-up to this lesson is to explore how authors explain terms like **segregation, racism, prejudice**. Some author's definitions are limited or constrained, while others suggest systemic oppression and ongoing tribulation. Teach your students to be critical consumers of glossaries.

Launching the Lesson

Remind students that they already know a lot about glossaries.

You might say, "Researchers, linguists! You already know a lot about glossaries—tell your partner when have you noticed and used a glossary as you read, or made one as a writer? Hmm, I heard you say that glossaries are often at the back, and sometimes writers put words in a different color, or make them bold, so the reader knows to check the glossary. Marta Magellan does that in her book. You can go to the back of the text to find the glossary, and look these terms up. And some of you mentioned that in online texts or ebooks, you can click on the word, and it takes you to the glossary definition."

What are these imposters up to?

The monarch's bright colors are a warning to birds and frogs. "If you eat me, you'll be sorry!" Birds throw up if they gobble up a monarch. And they will learn a lesson. No more orange butterflies for them. Monarch colors are like a special shield announcing they carry poison in their bodies. They taste terrible to birds and frogs.

It's easy for people to think the look-alikes mimic or copy the monarchs to stay safe.

But do they?

Engagement—Investigation and Practice

Suggest that some authors do some tricky work in glossaries. Invite learners to investigate a more challenging glossary, and teach them to return to the text to read between the text and the glossary to approximate the meaning of the word and that part of the text.

Introduce the trickier parts as an inquiry. "As you begin to read more complicated texts, you'll notice that the glossaries become trickier. Let's look at this section of the glossary from *Up, Up and Away, Monarchs*. Tell your partner, what are some tricky parts here?"

> **Mimicry** in biology a way unrelated organisms copy each other so that predators leave them alone.
>
> **Batesian Mimicry** the harmless one copies the colors of the dangerous one.
>
> **Müllerian Mimicry** the look-alike dangerous ones mutually benefit from their similar appearance, such as monarch butterflies and viceroy butterflies.
>
> ***Ophryocystis elektroscirrha*** scientific name for the protozoan parasite that affects monarch butterflies, called OE for short

Listen in, then coach students. "There are a lot of ways this glossary is tricky. One, it has Latin! Don't be afraid of Latin. If you can say **Tyrannosaurus Rex**, you can learn Latin! Two, there are technical scientific words, like **organism** or **parasites** inside the definitions. So, researchers, usually you need to *go back to the text*, find where the word was introduced, and then read around the word. See if there are more context clues *in the text*, and combine those with what you can decipher in the definition, and then you'll get closer to understanding the meaning of the word and, more importantly, that part of the text. Try that now with mimicry, or mimic—what do Marta and Mauro teach you about how other butterflies mimic the Monarch? Look at the pictures, read the paragraph—why is **mimicry** important? Use the glossary *and* the text, and explain to your partner."

The Look-Alikes

Viceroy butterfly

Soldier butterfly

Passion butterfly (Gulf fritillary)

Queen butterfly

They might be monarch copycats.

Some butterflies sport the exact same colors and even similar patterns. Look at the pictures of the look-alike butterflies. They can fool you into thinking they're monarchs.

What are these imposters up to?

The monarch's bright colors are a warning to birds and frogs. "If you eat me, you'll be sorry!" Birds throw up if they gobble up a monarch. And they will learn a lesson. No more orange butterflies for them. Monarch colors are like a special shield announcing they carry poison in their bodies. They taste terrible to birds and frogs.

It's easy for people to think the look-alikes mimic or copy the monarchs to stay safe.

But do they?

Application

Encourage learners to try this work out in all the texts they are reading, including digital texts. Remind them that what matters is that they understand what that part of the text teaches, and they can try to explain why the word matters (more important than a definition). Also encourage students to become glossary creators, in their notes and as writers.

You might say, "Linguists! You are ready to tackle not just tricky words but also more challenging texts, because you are willing to take the time to study the hard words, and use a tool like a glossary wisely. You won't be discouraged by a tricky glossary—you'll move back and forth between the text and the definition, so you understand what that part of the text teaches. And do this work as writers, too! You can be glossary creators!"

The work students will create during and after the lesson might look like ...

Writers create glossaries in their published writing, mimicking the mentor texts they've studied

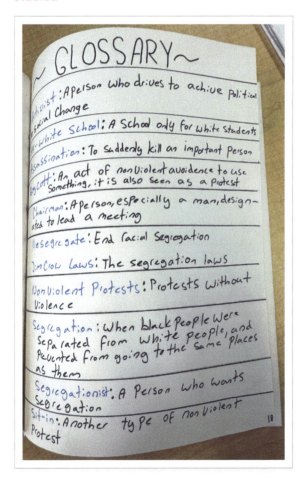

Researchers add glossaries to their notes

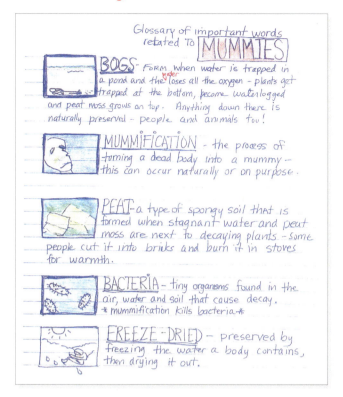

Glossary of important words related to MUMMIES

BOGS - Form when water is trapped in a pond and the water loses all the oxygen - plants get trapped at the bottom, become waterlogged and peat moss grows on top. Anything down there is naturally preserved - people and animals too!

MUMMIFICATION - the process of turning a dead body into a mummy - this can occur naturally or on purpose.

PEAT - a type of spongy soil that is formed when stagnant water and peat moss are next to decaying plants - some people cut it into bricks and burn it in stoves for warmth.

BACTERIA - tiny organisms found in the air, water and soil that cause decay.
* mummification kills bacteria *

FREEZE-DRIED - preserved by freezing the water a body contains, then drying it out.

Researchers add color coding to note important terms in their notes

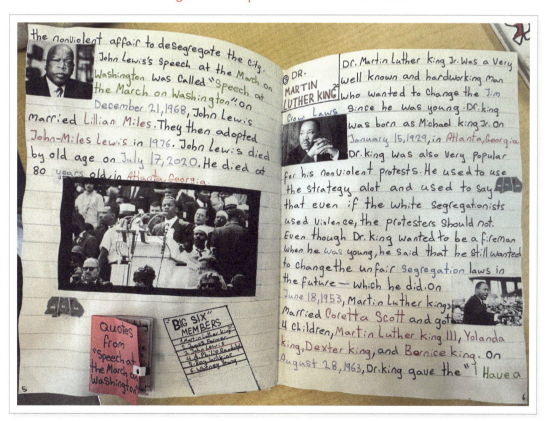

Tucked-In Definitions

Considerations

Lesson summary: In this session you'll teach students that writers don't always bold words and send readers to a glossary. Often, they tuck in definitions, in parentheses, between commas, often right after they introduce a new term. Sometimes they provide synonyms in the text, before or after they introduce a new term. You'll teach your readers to be alert for these tucked-in definitions, and to pause to think, "What is the meaning here? Not just of the word, but of this part of the text?" You'll invite your readers to practice on some excerpts from *Up, Up and Away, Monarchs*.

This work will support your students in noticing more nuanced context clues, so that they are not looking only for highlighted vocabulary words in the text. It will also support their rereading and deep comprehension skills.

Estimated lesson time: 10 minutes.

Materials and preparation: You'll need excerpts from *Up, Up and Away, Monarchs* or a text related to content students are studying. Choose snippets with tucked-in definitions, including one that is not immediately after the word.

Additional lesson options: It can be interesting to study the grammar of tucked-in definitions—the parenthetical phrases and appositives, which mirrors how fiction writers tuck in secrets about characters between parentheses or commas. In a narrative, for instance, the author might write: the powerful Monarch butterfly (who travels hundreds of miles in one lifetime) ... or the powerful Monarch butterfly (named after Prince William of Orange). Teach your students to study their texts as mentors, and to apply these same grammatical structures in their writing, using parenthetical phrases and appositives to say more.

Launching the Lesson

Suggest that readers be alert to how authors tuck in definitions, often between commas and parentheses. Invite students to study an accessible example.

You might say, "Researchers, authors don't always put new words in bold, or define them in glossaries. Sometimes they tuck in definitions, often between

> **Monarch butterflies are nature's wonder.**
>
> Legend has it that early settlers to North America admired the monarch's bright orange color. It made them think of Prince William of Orange who became a king. So they gave the butterfly the name monarch, which means ruler or king.

commas or parentheses. Take a look at this section of *Up, Up and Away, Monarchs*. Tell your partner, where do you see a tucked-in definition? What does it explain? I hear you saying that Marta tucks in a definition for **monarch**. She tells you that it means **ruler** or **king**."

Engagement—Investigation and Practice

Invite students to investigate a trickier tucked-in definition, one that is not placed exactly after the term. Encourage them to reread that part of the text, to notice clues the author gives the reader, such as synonyms, and to explain the term's significance in the text.

You might say, "Researchers, sometimes the author doesn't make the tucked-in definition as obvious—it's not right after the word. Then, you need to reread that part of the text, looking for clues the author has given you. Let's try that now. Let's go back to the page of the text you studied yesterday, when you were using the glossary to learn more about how some butterflies **mimic** the Monarch. This time, see if you can figure out what the word **imposter** means—and more importantly, explain why it's important, to understanding the role of **imposter** butterflies."

The Look-Alikes

Viceroy butterfly

Soldier butterfly

Passion butterfly (Gulf fritillary)

Queen butterfly

They might be monarch copycats.

Some butterflies sport the exact same colors and even similar patterns. Look at the pictures of the look-alike butterflies. They can fool you into thinking they're monarchs.

What are these imposters up to?

The monarch's bright colors are a warning to birds and frogs. "If you eat me, you'll be sorry!" Birds throw up if they gobble up a monarch. And they will learn a lesson. No more orange butterflies for them. Monarch colors are like a special shield announcing they carry poison in their bodies. They taste terrible to birds and frogs.

It's easy for people to think the look-alikes mimic or copy the monarchs to stay safe.

But do they?

You can summarize if needed, saying, "Some of you notice that Marta and Mauro give you a lot of context clues here. They tuck in a synonym, **copycat**! A nice compound word, too, copycat. And they give you a lot of illustrations of these **copycats**, these **imposters**. And they tuck in a definition in the paragraph before the word **imposter**. Marta explains that these are **look-alike** butterflies with the same colors and patterns. So interesting."

Application

Encourage learners to be flexible as they approach new vocabulary, to look not only for a glossary but also for tucked-in definitions. Suggest that they can also use this technique as writers, to explain expert vocabulary to their readers.

You might say, "Linguists! Use what you've learned as researchers and writers going forward! When you're researching, pay close attention to how authors tuck in synonyms and definitions, and how you can read around that part of the text to figure out the significance of a term. And try this out as writers—teach your audience new vocabulary by explaining expert terms in the text!"

The work students will create during and after the lesson might look like ...

This young writer teaches vocabulary with tucked-in definitions and a text feature

Marking up texts helps readers notice context clues and focus on bigger meanings

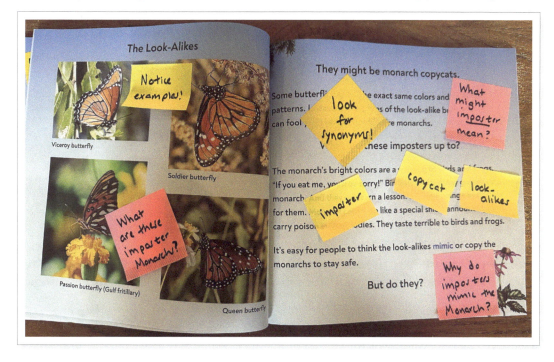

Context Is Everything

Considerations

Lesson summary: In this session you'll coach your students to pay attention to context as they figure out the meaning of domain vocabulary. You'll teach students that a lot of content vocabulary has multiple meanings, and that truly, context is everything. An **imposter** butterfly is similar but not quite the same as a human **imposter**. Similarly, **mimicry** has a particular scientific meaning when it is used to describe organisms. You'll alert children to the idea of secondary and specialized meanings, and you'll coach them to reread parts of the text and think about the meaning of content vocabulary in the context of the topic they are studying.

This work has immediate relevance for test prep. Almost all of the vocabulary questions on high-stakes ELA assessments are contextual. Often the word has a familiar meaning, and unwary readers are lured by that, when they need to return to the part of the text and consider context.

Estimated lesson time: 10 minutes.

Materials and preparation: You'll use a small excerpt from *Up, Up and Away, Monarch Butterflies*, or a text related to content your students are studying. Look for vocabulary words with meanings that shift depending on the context and content being studied.

Visit the website www.vocabularyconnections.org to download a chart of words with secondary meanings.

Additional lesson options: You may want to reteach this lesson if you teach a test prep unit. Teach students to reread the relevant part of the text, and to ask themselves: what does this word or phrase mean *in this context*?

Launching the Lesson

Present your readers with some words that have secondary meanings, and invite them to try to create contextual examples that demonstrate different meanings.

For example, you might say, "Linguists! Some vocabulary words have more than one meaning. Here are some examples—with your partner, try to give an example that would change the meaning of the word. For instance, I could say that I have a **solution** to your problem. Or you could say that you made a **solution** of water and sugar to feed hummingbirds. The word **solution** has different meanings, depending on context! Here are a few others—see what examples you can come up with and work with your partner to demonstrate the different meanings!"

ring	field	spring
current	row	bat

Engagement—Investigation and Practice

Invite students to look closely at the meaning of a word from the text. Start with the non-scientific meaning of the word and then pay close attention to the textual context.

You might say, "Let's try this work out now with a vocabulary term from *Up, Up and Away, Monarch Butterflies*. Marta Magellan uses the word **mimic**. First, tell your partner—if you **mimic** someone at recess, or when you're playing a sport, what does that mean? What might be an example?"

Summarize, saying, "When a soccer player tries to **mimic** a really good soccer player, they want to learn to be just like that player. Or a bully can **mimic** someone to be mean. So when people mimic, they can do it for different reasons. Let's see what Marta says it means to **mimic** in biology. She gives this definition …"

> **Mimicry** in biology a way unrelated organisms copy each other so that predators leave them alone.

Marta presents the idea of **mimicry** when she teaches you about the copycat, look-alike butterflies. What does it mean for a butterfly to **mimic** another butterfly? How is it different from the baseball player or the bully?

The Look-Alikes

Viceroy butterfly

Soldier butterfly

Passion butterfly (Gulf fritillary)

Queen butterfly

Application

Encourage students to pay close attention to context—to ask "What does this term mean in this context?" whenever they are reading.

You might say, "Whenever you are researching, think about what specific words mean in that context. In fact, you can do this same thing no matter what you are reading! Are you reading about the **bat** used in baseball or the **bat** who eats mosquitoes?"

The work students will create during and after the lesson might look like ...

Collecting words with specialized, secondary science meanings

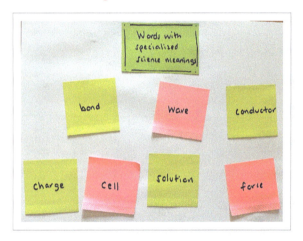

Collecting Spanish words with multiple meanings

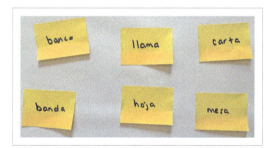

Tricky Text Features

Considerations

Lesson summary: In this session you'll teach students that authors use text features to *explain* and *illustrate* domain vocabulary and concepts. You'll invite your learners to join you in an investigation of how text features in a book offer opportunities to deepen understanding of a topic and of particular words and concepts. One note—in simpler texts, text features often offer an explicit definition of a term in the text. In more complex texts, however, the text features are often charts and diagrams that illustrate an important concept. These trickier text features may include several expert domain terms so the reader needs to study the entire text feature carefully.

This work supports students' vocabulary acquisition, leading them to pay closer attention to the information presented in text features. It supports their reading comprehension and knowledge building too, as many complex texts include complicated charts and diagrams that explain a lot of technical vocabulary and teach a lot of content.

Estimated lesson time: 10 minutes.

Materials and preparation: You'll need to demonstrate using nonfiction texts—*Up, Up and Away, Monarch Butterflies*, by Marta Magellan and Mauro Magellan. Of course, you can substitute any print text related to your content, but keep in mind that the first text feature should include information that learners have already studied, so they can study how the author uses this text feature. The second may be newer, more challenging vocabulary and features.

Additional lesson options: A powerful follow-up to this lesson includes teaching your readers how often, in more complex nonfiction, the text features don't make the text easier; instead they layer more and often complicated information. Explaining a visual in a science text, for instance, is a way for learners to articulate what they are learning about the topic. You might teach your learners, therefore, when they finish a text, to summarize by choosing an especially significant image, chart, or diagram, and explaining it to their partner, using the expert domain vocabulary they've learned in their explanation.

Another good lesson that reinforces prior learning is to remind students of the work they did with concept mapping (Chapter 5, Lesson 5.6). Often, more complex diagrams in nonfiction will be concept maps that demonstrate a sophisticated concept, and the relationship between expert terms. The captions can also be very helpful. Teach your students to be alert to these features as readers, and to study them as mentor texts as writers, and they'll increase their linguistic competencies dramatically.

Note: For a lot of your multilingual learners, the concept of multiple generations of migration will be one they have a deep personal understanding of. You might invite learners to map their own migrations, to compare to those of the Monarch, and as a way of celebrating how humans and all kinds of creatures move across the planet in order to thrive.

Launching the Lesson

Explain how text features often illustrate important concepts and vocabulary, and invite students to study one that includes terms with which they are at least partially familiar. Call attention to the text feature, the domain vocabulary, the caption, and the bigger concept being illustrated.

You might say, "Researchers, linguists, one way that nonfiction authors teach their audience a lot of important words and concepts is through text features. When you were younger, the text features might have been a simple text box, with a definition—and you'll still find those. But you'll also find more complicated charts and diagrams that you need to study, to figure out not only the meaning of new words but also what the text feature illustrates. Often it's not just new words, it's a bigger concept or idea. Let's take a look at one together. It's from *Up, Up and Away, Monarch Butterflies*. As you study this chart with a partner, ask yourself these questions: What concept does this text feature explain? What important vocabulary does it illustrate?"

You can summarize and elevate what students say: "I hear you saying that this chart explains the life cycle of the Monarch butterfly. It illustrates how the **caterpillars** hatch from **eggs**. They form a **chrysalis**, from which the adult Monarch emerges. Some of you talked about the word **emerge**, and how this text feature shows the adult Monarch crawling out of the chrysalis. It **crawls out**, or **emerges**. What's also important is how all of you looked from the diagram to the caption below it. Always do that! In this case, you realized that this text feature teaches the reader a lot of important vocabulary and a big concept—how the Monarch butterfly changes across its life cycle!"

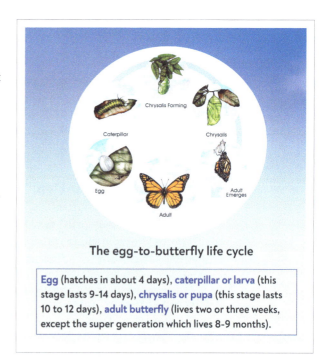

The egg-to-butterfly life cycle

Egg (hatches in about 4 days), **caterpillar or larva** (this stage lasts 9-14 days), **chrysalis or pupa** (this stage lasts 10 to 12 days), **adult butterfly** (lives two or three weeks, except the super generation which lives 8-9 months).

Engagement—Investigation and Practice

Invite students to try this work out again, with another, trickier text feature from the text (in this case, a complicated map showing several variables). Encourage them to go from the words of the text to the text feature and back, as a way to deepen their comprehension. Then invite them to explain the significance of the text feature and the vocabulary words it includes.

You might say, "Try this work again, this time on an even trickier text feature. In this one, Marta and Mauro use a text feature to explain two terms—**migration** and **instinct**. And they illustrate what it means for multiple **generations** of butterflies to **migrate**. Study this map, and the words next to it, and see if you can figure out what **migration** means, what **instinct** might mean, and what **first, second, third generation** means. Read across the image and the words, and try to explain to your partner."

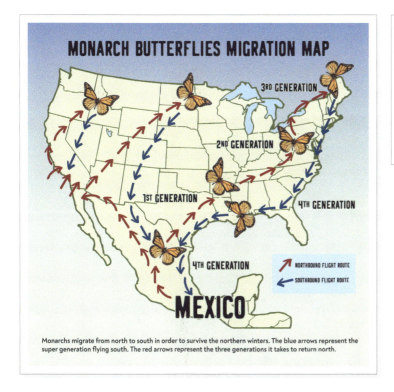

MONARCH BUTTERFLIES MIGRATION MAP

3RD GENERATION

2ND GENERATION

1ST GENERATION

4TH GENERATION

4TH GENERATION

MEXICO

↗ NORTHBOUND FLIGHT ROUTE
↙ SOUTHBOUND FLIGHT ROUTE

Monarchs migrate from north to south in order to survive the northern winters. The blue arrows represent the super generation flying south. The red arrows represent the three generations it takes to return north.

Migrating monarchs use instinct.

That means they are born knowing what to do. It's like they have a secret code in their brains guiding them. Instinct tells each generation things like how to travel along the flyway using the position of the sun. Instinct shows them how to lay eggs only on plants called milkweeds. It also leads them back to the birthplace of their great-great grandparents.

Coach students to use context clues and strategies, saying, "Notice the key on the map—use that! Think how this map is showing movement over land and movement of time. Use what you learned about tucked-in definitions too!"

Then summarize. "I hear you noticing that the author gives a tucked-in definition for **instinct**—it's a secret code in the butterflies' brains that guides them. And you figured out **migration**—traveling along the flyway. And you figured out **flyway**!"

Celebrate personal connections. "I also hear you thinking about how humans and monarchs **migrate** over **generations**!"

Application

Encourage students to use all their strategies to figure out and explain how complicated charts and diagrams they find as text features illustrate important vocabulary. Also encourage them to return to these as mentor texts when they write nonfiction.

You might say, "Writers, whenever you come upon a complicated chart or diagram in a text feature, pause and really study it. Look between the text feature and text, and really take your time to investigate the terms and concepts this text feature illustrates. Try to explain it to yourself or a partner. And come back to these as mentor texts when you are writing—your nonfiction writing will be so much more compelling when you try these same techniques to teach your audience important terms and concepts."

The work students will create during and after the lesson might look like ...

Explaining complex text features is a method for summarizing and applying expert vocabulary

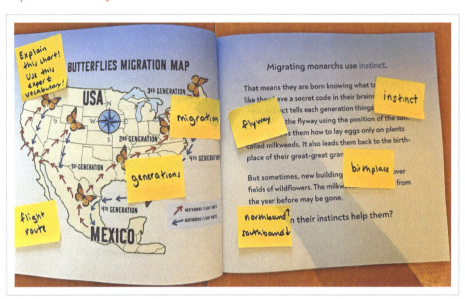

Semantic map inside a complex text feature

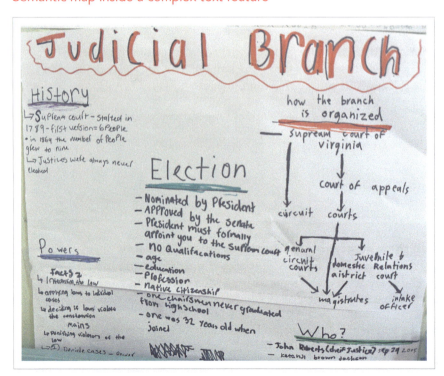

Lesson 6.5

Video Vocabulary

Considerations

Lesson summary: In this session you'll coach your students in paying attention to and learning vocabulary from content videos such as science and social studies. Video texts present a lot of information rapidly. You'll teach students to pay attention to what the narrator says, to visual images, and to pop-ups or graphics. You'll also suggest that turning on captions can be helpful. You'll practice this work with students, using butterfly videos, coaching them to figure out when the author is teaching important vocabulary and to jot vocabulary as a form of note taking.

This work is important to your students' overall digital reading competency. Video texts are engaging, and they present a huge amount of information at a rapid pace. It's easy to have the content wash over you. This strategy encourages learners to slow down, to reread, to note-take, as well as collect domain vocabulary.

Estimated lesson time: 10 minutes.

Materials and preparation: You'll need to show excerpts from science videos. The first video in this lesson is *Butterflies for Kids*, by LearnBright. This digital text includes pop-ups with written words, as a cue for the learner. The second video is *Monarch Butterflies*, by Amazing Animals for National Geographic for Kids. This text mostly relies on narration to introduce new terms. You can substitute similar videos related to other content you are studying with your students.

Additional lesson options: You can extend this lesson by applying it to podcasts and audio books as well as ebooks. Digital texts offer supports and challenges for comprehension. Learners tend to enjoy them, and taking away print comprehension can help students learn content in a different modality. And they need support to read deeply and cull important information and terms.

Launching the Lesson

Suggest to students that it's tricky to learn vocabulary from videos, because they move so quickly and we're often focused on the images. Invite them to practice the strategy of reading and rereading with the lens of vocabulary collection, paying close attention to all context clues, including narration, pop-ups, and images. Watch a snippet of *Butterflies for Kids*, by LearnBright.

You might say, "Researchers, it can be especially tricky to learn vocabulary from videos, even though they teach a lot of vocabulary. But they tend to move very quickly, and you have to pay attention to three things at the same time. It helps to read with a lens, saying to yourself: I am going to be alert to important vocabulary, and I'm going to pay attention to…"

- What the narrator is saying

- The images

- Any pop-ups or graphics

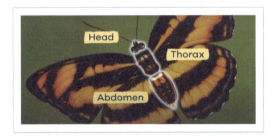

After you play a snippet of the video, you might summarize, saying, "In this video, a lot of you noticed how the authors include pop-ups, or graphics, that often let you know important vocabulary is being introduced, like the body parts of the butterfly, or the term **iridescence**."

Engagement—Investigation and Practice

Invite students to practice this work again, this time with a slightly harder video that doesn't include graphics. Suggest they jot vocabulary words as they come up, as a way of holding onto words and also information. Watch a snippet from Amazing Animals (National Geographic for Kids), *Monarch Butterflies*.

You might say, "Let's try this one more time, with a trickier video. In this one, there aren't as many graphics, which means you have to really listen to what the narrator says, and at the same time, see if the visuals help you understand what they say. I'll give you one tip: sometimes it helps to turn the captions on, so you can see some of the words. But you have to try that out—sometimes you only want captions on the second read, when you're rereading. Let's watch a little bit, and then reread with the captions on."

You can summarize again, tucking in tips. "Readers, rereading a bit with the captions was helpful. At first, we focused on how beautiful this butterfly is. But then the caption helped us recognize and jot down the word **milkweed**—which wasn't in a pop-up or graphic."

Application

Encourage students to slow down when they learn from videos—to reread with the lens of vocabulary, to jot notes, to use all the context clues to help them accumulate expert vocabulary and deepen their learning.

You might say, "Linguists! Whenever you are researching from a video, remember that you'll often want to read it more than once. On the second viewing, you can read with the lens of vocabulary, and you can use all the context clues to help you learn more and jot notes."

The work students will create during and after the lesson might look like ...

Researchers collect scientific vocabulary from digital texts

Nature videos allow learners to pause in order to sketch and label

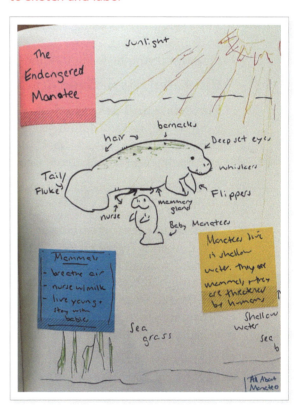

Word Choice Matters

Considerations

Lesson summary: In this session you'll teach your students to play close attention to word choice as a way to analyze tone. In particular, you'll suggest they pay close attention to the adjectives and verbs authors use, and think about whether these suggest how the author feels about the topic. For example, does the author describe pesticides as **necessary** or **damaging**? You'll return to a snippet from the National Geographic video you played yesterday and to an excerpt from *Up, Up and Away, Butterflies*.

This work supports young readers' skills with close and critical reading and with critical questioning. Paying close attention to word choice and tone is a technique for investigating authors' stances and points of view and for increasing criticality.

Estimated lesson time: 10 minutes.

Materials and preparation: You'll need to share some examples of sentences whose word choice creates a definite tone, for students to analyze. You'll also share some snippets from two texts—*Up, Up and Away, Monarch Butterflies*, and *Monarch Butterflies*, by Amazing Animals, National Geographic for Kids.

Visit the website www.vocabularyconnections.org to download sample sentences.

Additional lesson options: If you can, follow up on this lesson in social studies. The word choice in social studies texts are clues to the author's sympathies, stance, and point of view. Who do they describe as daring and brave? Who is described as rebellious or oppressive? Who is described as a hero and who is described as a victim? Often, the way individuals and groups of people are described is illuminating—and problematic. Learning to pay attention to and question word choice is one way to increase criticality.

Another lesson follow-up is to invite students to collect and compare authors who write on the same topic. When readers look across Seymour Simons's *Sharks* (1995), and Catherine Roy's gorgeous *Neighborhood Sharks* (2014), for example, and compare the word choice and tone in those to these same craft moves in Cathy East Dubowski's *Shark Attack!* (2009), they'll have a lot to say about word choice.

Launching the Lesson

Suggest that word choice creates a tone, and it gives readers clues about the author's stance or perspective—how they feel about the topic. Give a couple of examples for students to study.

You might say, "Linguists! You've learned so much about context clues, which is really all about close reading. Well, there is one more subtle context clue, and that is word choice, which will give you clues about how the author feels about the topic. Here are some examples. Try to describe the author's feelings about dung beetles, based on their word choice, the vocabulary they use."

Author A
Dung beetles are incredibly industrious creatures. They cleanse the earth of dung, or poop, doing an admirable service to all.

Author B
Dung beetles crawl in other animals' poop, eating this unappetizing food and sometimes bringing it home to their young. When you see these greedy creatures, you know that poop is nearby.

You might summarize children's observations, saying, "I heard you say that Author A seems to admire the dung beetle. They use words like **industrious, cleanse**, and **admirable**, whereas Author B seems to find them disgusting—they use words like **crawl, unappetizing**, and **greedy**! You're using literary vocabulary to describe their feelings, just like you did with *Joy and Heron*! And you figured out their feelings from the *tone* of the text."

Engagement—Investigation and Practice

Invite students to study a snippet of two texts (*Amazing Butterflies* and *Up, Up and Away, Monarch Butterflies*), and to practice analyzing them for tone by studying the author's word choice.

You might say, "Let's try this work out now with some of our butterfly texts. Here's a snippet from *Up, Up and Away, Monarch Butterflies*."

"And here's a snippet from the video *Monarch Butterflies—Amazing Animals*":

Monarchs are many people's favorite butterfly. They are the most studied, tracked, and recognized of all butterflies.

What makes them the celebrities of the insect world?

The Monarch begins its amazing transformation from a pupa to something truly magical.

"How would you describe each author's tone? How do they feel about Monarch butterflies—and what vocabulary is a clue?"

Again, you can summarize, saying something like, "I hear you saying that both authors seem to love the Monarch. Their word choice—words like **amazing, magical, favorite, celebrity**—creates a tone of **admiration** and **celebration**."

Application

Encourage students to carry this work forward, especially as a way to embrace criticality.

You might say, "Readers, try out this lens whenever you are reading nonfiction. It's powerful, for instance, in social studies to investigate an author's word choice as a way to figure out who they sympathize with. Some particular vocabulary words—often verbs and adjectives—give you clues about the author's point of view and feelings about the topic."

The work students will create during and after the lesson might look like ...

Investigating word choice in sample sentences

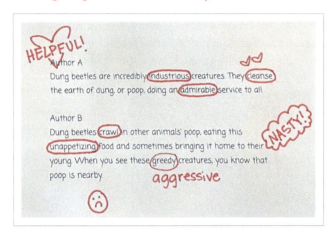

Analyzing word choice and tone

An anchor chart helps learners remember and transfer skills and habits

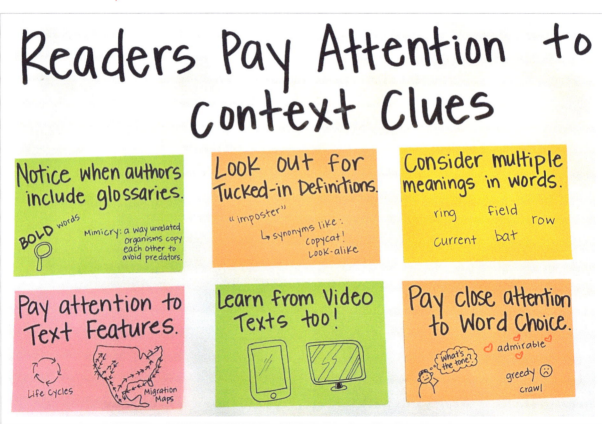

Conclusion
Continuing Vocabulary Connections Across Grade Levels and Learners

As you and your colleagues add structured vocabulary instruction to your existing curriculum, you'll find yourself wondering about grade-level decisions and multiple pathways for different kinds of learners. These are great conversations. Fortunately, you don't have to change instructional methods to make the work presented here more sophisticated by grade level, or to simplify it or extend it for groups of learners. Rather, the way you'll make modifications will mostly involve making thoughtful decisions about the range of vocabulary, the choice of texts, and the difficulty of the topics you'll dive into with your students. As you close this book and begin to think about how you'll incorporate and expand out from all you've learned, here are a few ways to think about these decisions and progressions.

Literary Vocabulary

The first way to shift the work around literary vocabulary to explore a greater range of words is to simply change the text itself. If, for instance, grade 3 launches this work with the Pixar video, *Joy and Heron*, grade 4 might continue it with the marvelous *Piper*, also a Pixar video, about a captivating young bird who learns self-sufficiency on the shoreline. Where grade 3 collected vocabulary around a few words to describe **joyful, curious, protective**, grade 4 might shift to including considerably more words to describe **helpless, naive, unprepared, persevering**. If grade 5 explores the short film, *Supporting Act*, about a father and daughter who come to see each other more fully, they could investigate words for **self-centered, overwhelmed, confident, dejected**. And if grade 6 explores the short film, *Lou*, about a boy who seems to be a schoolyard bully, they might find themselves charting words for **damaged, destructive, aggressive, penitent, lonely**.

Shifting to more complex narratives introduces more complex emotions and traits, and consequently more sophisticated vocabulary. You might, therefore, want to make some initial decisions with your colleagues about which digital texts you'll use for each grade level. Know that every year, there will be new and compelling digital texts to choose from.

Another way to contain or extend children's initial investigations of literary vocabulary is to consider the number, range, and level of words you introduce. If you are introducing a vertical for **happy** to a group of newcomers, for instance, you might begin with simply **pleased—happy—joyful**, rather than **pleased—happy—delighted—content—gleeful—joyful—euphoric**. Inside of this deliberation, you can consider Tier 1, Tier 2, and Tier 3 words. Tier 1 words like **happy** are useful for anchoring new words for learners. Tier 2 words like **joyful** and **delighted** will be useful as children expand their vocabulary—and their reading. Tier 3 literary words, rarer words like

blithe, may be extension opportunities you offer your avid readers and word collectors. Note, these decisions don't need to be limited to grade levels. You'll have readers who are ready for more words and more sophisticated word choices in any grade, and you can support these readers in small group work, offering new and more extensive verticals.

Word Consciousness

As you teach etymology, compound words, cognates, and morphology, you can also think about grade-level choices and small group work. Some of your budding historians and language scholars will love to learn about Anglo-Saxon derivations as compared to Greek and Latin. They'll enjoy sorting words by their likely history, and thinking about the implications of patterns they notice. In the same way, your multilingual learners who speak languages derived from Latin will be poised to capitalize on cognates, as so very many words will be similar. And some of your learners will, quite simply, fall in love with morphology. They'll love learning about the parts of words as they begin to notice these parts whenever they read and their understanding of word meanings soars.

If you can, sit with your vertical grade-level colleagues to make some decisions about which prefixes, suffixes, and roots you'll introduce and review in each grade level. You're going to be able to go farther and teach more when you work with an awareness of what children studied the year before. Visit classrooms to see each other's word charts. Discuss what you're noticing instructionally. Ask questions of one another. Share your overall plan. Of course, you can always make your own list and plan—but doing this with colleagues maximizes efficiency, cohesion, and likelihood of transfer.

Domain Vocabulary

With domain vocabulary, the range of vocabulary children learn is going to shift as you explore new topics in different grade levels, especially topics in social studies and science. You can make modifications for newcomers and multilingual learners, especially by including new vocabulary in multiple languages. Be careful not to assume that these learners aren't ready for Tier 2 and Tier 3 words in content studies—precise and specialized science and social studies words will be new for all your learners. If they have accessible and compelling texts, and multiple experiences collecting and talking about new words, your multilingual learners will learn highly technical vocabulary. Indeed, making sure that learners understand the context and significance of new conceptual vocabulary will also mean you are making sure the curriculum itself is meaningful to all your students.

One area that you might differentiate will be in note taking. For students who take a long time to write, sketching and labeling may serve as a primary note-taking method, and conceptual vocabulary sorts will launch lively content discussions, while for older students and more proficient writers, jotting captions, creating glossaries, and engaging in more elaborate note taking will create more opportunities to deepen and extend their domain vocabulary and content knowledge, as well as their ability to explain their new understandings to others.

One last tip. Start to develop your own awareness of language! Learn new words and languages from your students. Start paying attention to how many cognates exist for the languages your students speak. Use AI to learn more. Notice how morphology might help you and your students figure out word meanings as you read aloud, explore a shared text, or come upon a new word. Collect authors who love words. Set kids up to be **entomologists** and **meteorologists** and **archaeologists**. Fall in love with expert science words. Notice when a child knows words like **Velociraptor** and **Spinosaurus**! Notice, as well, when an author calls a historical figure **rebellious** or **defiant** versus **courageous** and **committed**. Criticality, word consciousness, and love of language are contagious.

And once learners start to make these vocabulary connections, you'll be amazed at the readers and writers they become. Thoughtful. Engaged. Confident. And overflowing with word consciousness and word knowledge they can't wait to share!

Children's Literature, Nonfiction, and Media References

Digital Narratives

BBC One Christmas 2017 | The Supporting Act, 2017. www.youtube.com/watch?v=8PstSiTCk74.

CGI Animated Short Film HD "Dust Buddies" by Beth Tomashek & Sam Wade | CGMeetup, 2016. www.youtube.com/watch?v=mZ6eeAjgSZI.

CGI Animated Short Film "Joy and Heron" by Passion Pictures | CGMeetup, 2018. https://www.youtube.com/watch?v=1lo-8UWhVcg&t=8s.

Hair Love | Oscar®-Winning Short Film (Full) | Sony Pictures Animation, 2019. www.youtube.com/watch?v=kNw8V_Fkw28.

Lou, 2017. www.youtube.com/watch?v=Q8MS4LLlv8Y.

Pip | A Short Animated Film by Dogs Inc, 2018. https://www.youtube.com/watch?v=07d2dXHYb94.

Piper, 2016. www.youtube.com/watch?v=PVYjvDKlV-w.

Narrative Picture Books

Barnes, Derrick. *Crown: An Ode to the Fresh Cut*. Illustrated by Gordon C. James. Chicago: Agate Bolden, 2017.

Flett, Julie. *Birdsong*. Vancouver: Greystone Kids, 2019.

Ludwig, Trudy. *The Invisible Boy*. Illustrated by Patrice Barton. New York: Knopf Books for Young Readers, 2013.

Medina, Meg. *Evelyn Del Rey Is Moving Away*. Illustrated by Sonia Sánchez. Somerville, Massachusetts: Candlewick, 2020.

Peña, Matt de la. *Last Stop on Market Street*. Illustrated by Christian Robinson. New York, NY: G.P. Putnam's Sons Books for Young Readers, 2015.

Quang, Phùng Nguyên, and Huynh Kim Liên. *My First Day*. New York: Make Me a World, 2021.

Quintero, Isabel. *My Papi Has a Motorcycle*. Illustrated by Zeke Peña. New York: Kokila, 2019.

Ramadan, Danny. *Salma the Syrian Chef*. Illustrated by Anna Bron. Toronto, Ontario: Annick Press, 2020.

Scott, Jordan. *I Talk Like a River*. Illustrated by Sydney Smith. New York: Neal Porter Books, 2020.

Wang, Andrea, and Jason Chin. *Watercress*. Illustrated by Jason Chin. New York: Holiday House, 2022.

Nonfiction

Dubowski, Cathy East. *Shark Attack*! DK Readers. New York: DK Publishing, 2009.

Hayakawa, S.I., Alan R. Hayakawa, and Robert MacNeil. *Language in Thought and Action: Fifth Edition*. 1st ed. San Diego: Harvest Original, 1991.

Learn Bright. *Butterflies for Kids | Learn about the Diet, Habitat, and Behaviors of Butterflies*, 2023. "https://www.youtube.com/watch?v=J8aYreaXkHo" https://www.youtube.com/watch?v=J8aYreaXkHo.

Learn Bright. *Life Cycle of a Butterfly | Butterflies for Kids | Learn the 4 Stages of the Butterfly Life Cycle*, 2020. "https://www.youtube.com/watch?v=PWi-dQ-FMB8" https://www.youtube.com/watch?v=PWi-dQ-FMB8.

Magellan, Marta. *Up, Up and Away, Monarch Butterflies*. Illustrated by Mauro Magellan, with photographs by James Gersing. Lemont, PA: Eifrig Publishing, 2024.

National Geographic for Kids - Amazing Animals. *Butterflies for Kids | Learn about the Diet, Habitat, and Behaviors of Butterflies*, 2023. "https://www.youtube.com/watch?v=J8aYreaXkHo" https://www.youtube.com/watch?v=J8aYreaXkHo.

National Geographic Kids. "Monarch Butterfly." Animals, 2024. "https://kids.nationalgeographic.com/animals/invertebrates/facts/monarch-butterfly" https://kids.nationalgeographic.com/animals/invertebrates/facts/monarch-butterfly.

Roy, Katherine. *Neighborhood Sharks: Hunting with the Great Whites of California's Farallon Islands*. First edition. New York: David Macaulay Studio, Roaring Brook Press, 2014.

Simon, Seymour. *Sharks*. New York: Harper Collins, 1995.

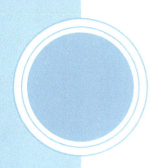

Academic References

Ahmed, Sarah. *Being the Change: Lessons and Strategies to Teach Social Comprehension*. Portsmouth, NH: Heinemann, 2018.

Ajayi, Lasisi. "Meaning-Making, Multimodal Representation, and Transformative Pedagogy: An Exploration of Meaning Construction Instructional Practices in an ESL High School Classroom." *Journal of Language, Identity & Education* 7, no. 3–4 (August 19, 2008): 206–29.

Alhassan, Bawa, and Mavis Osei. "Effectiveness of Integrating Drawing in Teaching English Language in Intellectual Disability Classroom." *International Journal on Social and Education Sciences* 4, no. 1 (January 15, 2022): 74–86.

Beck, Isabel L., Margaret G. McKeown, Linda Kucan, Margaret G. McKeown, and Linda Kucan. *Bringing Words to Life: Robust Vocabulary Instruction*. 2nd ed. New York: Guilford Press, 2013.

Cabell, Sonia. "Choosing and Using Complex Text: Every Student, Every Day." Massachusetts Department of Elementary and Secondary Education, 2022. www.doe.mass.edu/massliteracy/literacy-block/complex-text/choosing-using.html.

Cárdenas-Hagan, Elsa. *Literacy Foundations for English Learners: A Comprehensive Guide to Evidence-Based Instruction*. 1st ed. Brookes Publishing, 2020.

Carlo, María S., Diane August, Barry Mclaughlin, Catherine E. Snow, Cheryl Dressler, David N. Lippman, Teresa J. Lively, and Claire E. White. "Closing the Gap: Addressing the Vocabulary Needs of English-language Learners in Bilingual and Mainstream Classrooms." *Reading Research Quarterly* 39, no. 2 (April 6, 2004): 188–215.

Carnegie Corporation of New York. "Writing to Read: Evidence for How Writing Can Improve Reading." Carnegie Corporation of New York, 2010. www.carnegie.org/publications/writing-to-read-evidence-for-how-writing-can-improve-reading/.

Carter, Nichole. *Sketchnoting in the Classroom: A Practical Guide to Deepen Student Learning*. 1st ed. Portland, OR: International Society for Technology in Education, 2019.

Cenoz, Jasone, Oihana Leonet, and Durk Gorter. "Developing Cognate Awareness through Pedagogical Translanguaging." *International Journal of Bilingual Education and Bilingualism* 25, no. 8 (September 14, 2022): 2759–73.

Cherry-Paul, Sonja. *Antiracist Reading Revolution (Grades K-8): A Framework for Teaching Beyond Representation toward Liberation*. Thousand Oaks, CA: Corwin, 2024.

Clark, Roy Peter. *Writing Tools: 55 Essential Strategies for Every Writer*. Revised Little, Brown paperback edition. 10th anniversary ed. New York: Little, Brown and Company, 2016.

"Classroom Vocabulary Assessment for Content Areas" | Reading Rockets. Accessed March 15, 2024. www.readingrockets.org/topics/assessment-and-evaluation/articles/classroom-vocabulary-assessment-content-areas.

Cunningham, Katie Egan, Jan Miller Burkins, and Kari Yates. *Shifting the Balance: 6 Ways to Bring the Science of Reading into the Upper Elementary Classroom*. Portsmouth, NH: Stenhouse Publishers, 2023.

Duke, Nell, and P. David Pearson. "Effective Practices for Developing Reading Comprehension." *What Research Has to Say about Reading Instruction* 3 (January 1, 2002).

Duke, Nell K., Alessandra E. Ward, and P. David Pearson. "The Science of Reading Comprehension Instruction." *The Reading Teacher* 74, no. 6 (2021): 663–72.

Eduardo Briceño: How to Get Better at the Things You Care About, 2017. www.youtube.com/watch?v=YKACzIrog24.

Ehrenworth, Mary, Lauren Gould, and Alexandra Roman. "Joyful Vocabulary Acquisition: Pedagogies for Developing Children's Literary Vocabulary (and Analysis of Characters in Narratives)." In *Multiliteracies, Multimodality and Learning by (Inclusive) Design in Second Language Teacher Education*, edited by Agustín Reyes-Torres, María Estela Brisk, and Manel Lacorte. London: Routledge, 2025.

Ehrenworth, Mary, Pablo Wolfe, and Marc Todd. *The Civically Engaged Classroom: Reading, Writing, and Speaking for Change*. 1st ed. Portsmouth, NH: Heinemann, 2020.

España, Carla, and Luz Yadira Herrera. *En Comunidad: Lessons for Centering the Voices and Experiences of Bilingual Latinx Students*. Portsmouth, NH: Heinemann, 2020.

Espinosa, Cecilia M., and Laura Ascenzi-Moreno. *Rooted in Strength: Using Translanguaging to Grow Multilingual Readers and Writers*. New York: Scholastic, 2021.

García, Ofelia, Susana Ibarra Johnson, Kate Seltzer, and Guadalupe Valdés. *The Translanguaging Classroom: Leveraging Student Bilingualism for Learning*. Philadelphia, PA: Caslon, 2017.

Hakim, Joy, ed. *All the People: Since 1945*. 4th ed. New York: Oxford University Press, 2010.

Helman, Lori. *Literacy Development with English Learners: Research-Based Instruction in Grades K-6*. 2nd ed. New York: Guilford Press, 2016.

Hiebert, Elfrieda H. "Growing Capacity with Literary Vocabulary: The Megaclusters Framework." *American Reading Forum Yearbook* 31 (January 1, 2011).

Hiebert, Elfrieda H. *Teaching Words and How They Work: Small Changes for Big Vocabulary Results*. New York: Teachers College Press, 2020.

Hiebert, Elfrieda H., and David P. Pearson. *Generative Vocabulary Instruction*. ReadyGen., Pearson, 2013.

Hogan, Tiffany P., Suzanne M. Adlof, and Crystle Alonzo. "On the Importance of Listening Comprehension." *International Journal of Speech-Language Pathology* 16, no. 3 (June 2014): 199–207.

Howard, Jaleel R., Tanya Milner-McCall, and Tyrone C. Howard. *Not This But That: No More Teaching Without Positive Relationships*. Portsmouth, NH: Heinemann, 2020.

Kalantzis, Mary, Bill Cope, Eveline Chan, and Leanne Dalley-Trim. *Literacies*. 2nd ed. Port Melbourne, VIC, Australia: Cambridge University Press, 2016.

Kelly, Ronan, and Heng Hou. "Empowering Learners of English as an Additional Language: Translanguaging with Machine Translation." *Language and Education* 36, no. 6 (November 1, 2022): 544–59.

Lake, Vickie E., and Amber H. Beisly. "Translation Apps: Increasing Communication with Dual Language Learners." *Early Childhood Education Journal* 47, no. 4 (July 1, 2019): 489–96.

Lems, Kristin, Tenena M. Soro, and Gareth Charles. *Building Literacy with Multilingual Learners: Insights from Linguistics*. 3rd ed. New York: Guilford Press, 2024.

"Margaret McKeown Discusses Research on Vocabulary Assessment." *AERA*. 2015. www.youtube.com/watch?v=49vxKZcj7dY.

Martínez-Álvarez, Patricia. *Teaching Emergent Bilingual Students with Dis/Abilities: Humanizing Pedagogies to Engage Learners and Eliminate Labels*. Disability, Culture, and Equity Series. New York: Teachers College Press, 2023.

McCrum, Robert, William Cran, and Robert MacNeil. *The Story of English*. 3., rev. ed. New York: Penguin Books, 2003.

McGovern Institute. *Beyond the 30 Million Word Gap*, 2018. www.youtube.com/watch?v=CNJQGbNbI-8.

Medina, Meg. *Evelyn Del Rey Is Moving Away*. Illustrated by Sonia Sánchez. Somerville, MA: Candlewick, 2020.

Moll, Luis C., and Norma González. "Lessons from Research with Language-Minority Children." *Journal of Reading Behavior* 26, no. 4 (December 1994): 439–56.

Muhammad, Gholdy. *Unearthing Joy: A Guide to Culturally and Historically Responsive Teaching and Learning*. New York: Scholastic Inc, 2023.

Pajor, Allison. "What Should Morphology Instruction Look Like?" *IMSE—Journal*, July 25, 2023. https://journal.imse.com/what-should-morphology-instruction-look-like/.

Parks, Rosa, and James Haskins. *Rosa Parks: My Story*. New York, Puffin Books, 1999.

Pearson, P. David, Palincsar, Annemarie Sullivan, Biancarosa, Gina, and Berman, Amy I., eds. *Reaping the Rewards of the Reading for Understanding Initiative*. Washington, DC: National Academy of Education, 2020. https://naeducation.org/reaping-the-rewards-of-reading-for-understanding-initiative/.

Reyes-Torres, Agustín, and Matilde Portalés Raga. "A Multimodal Approach to Foster the Multiliteracies Pedagogy in the Teaching of EFL through Picturebooks: The Snow Lion." *Atlantis. Journal of the Spanish Association for Anglo-American Studies* 42, no. 1 (June 28, 2020): 94–119.

Romeo, Rachel R., Julia A. Leonard, Sydney T. Robinson, Martin R. West, Allyson P. Mackey, Meredith L. Rowe, and John D. E. Gabrieli. "Beyond the 30-Million-Word Gap: Children's Conversational Exposure Is Associated with Language-Related Brain Function." *Psychological Science* 29, no. 5 (May 1, 2018): 700–10.

Schwartz, Katrina. "Why Teachers Are So Excited About the Power of Sketchnoting—MindShift," *KQED*, November 4, 2019. www.kqed.org/mindshift/54655/why-teachers-are-so-excited-about-the-power-of-sketchnoting.

Sedita, Joan. "Using Morphology to Teach Vocabulary." *Keys to Literacy*, December 6, 2018. https://keystoliteracy.com/blog/using-morphology-to-teach-vocabulary/.

Shanahan, Tim. "How I Teach Students to Use Context in Vocabulary Learning" | Reading Rockets, 2023. Accessed July 5, 2024. www.readingrockets.org/blogs/shanahan-on-literacy/how-i-teach-students-use-context-vocabulary-learning.

Shanahan, Tim. "What Should Morphology Instruction Look Like?" | Reading Rockets. 2018. Accessed March 15, 2024. www.readingrockets.org/blogs/shanahan-on-literacy/what-should-morphology-instruction-look.

"The Vocabulary-Rich Classroom: Modeling Sophisticated Word Use to Promote Word Consciousness and Vocabulary Growth" | Reading Rockets. Accessed March 15, 2024. www.readingrockets.org/topics/vocabulary/articles/vocabulary-rich-classroom-modeling-sophisticated-word-use-promote-word.

Tutt, Paige. "How—and Why—to Introduce Visual Note-Taking to Your Students." Edutopia, April 9, 2021. www.edutopia.org/article/how-and-why-introduce-visual-note-taking-your-students/.

Vogel, Sara, and Ofelia García. "Translanguaging." *Oxford Research Encyclopedia of Education*, December 1, 2017.

Wood, Carla L., Christopher Schatschneider, and Allyssa VelDink. "The Relation Between Academic Word Use and Reading Comprehension for Students from Diverse Backgrounds." *Language, Speech, and Hearing Services in Schools* 52, no. 1 (January 19, 2021): 273–87.

Zapata, Gabriela C. *Learning by Design and Second Language Teaching: Theory, Research, and Practice*. London: Routledge, 2022.

Zucker, Tricia A., Sonia Q. Cabell, and Danielle L. Pico. "Going Nuts for Words: Recommendations for Teaching Young Students Academic Vocabulary." *The Reading Teacher* 74, no. 5 (2021): 581–94.

Credits

Illustrations by Jennifer Zanghi

Chapter 2

Cover of *Writing to Read: Evidence for How Writing Can Improve Reading* by Steve Graham and Michael Hebert. © 2010 by Carnegie Corporation of New York

Cover and interior spread of *Evelyn del Ray Is Moving Away*. Text copyright © 2020 by Meg Medina. Illustrations copyright © 2020 by Sonia Sanchez. Reproduced by permission of the publisher, Candlewick Press.

Cover of *My Papi Has a Motorcycle* by Isabel Quintero. Illustrated by Zeke Pena. © 2019 Penguin Random House Publishing.

Cover of *Salma the Syrian Chef*. Text © 2020 by Danny Ramadan. Illustrations © 2020 by Anna Bron. Reproduced by permission of the publisher, Annick Press.

Cover of *Birdsong* by Julie Flett. © 2019. Reproduced by permission of the publisher, Greystone Kids.

Cover of *The Invisible Boy* by Trudy Ludwig. Illustrated by Patrice Barton © 2013 Penguin Random House Publishing.

Cover of *My First Day* by Phùng Nguyên Quang and Huynh Kim Liên. Illustrated by Gordon C. James. © 2021 Penguin Random House Publishing.

Cover of *Crown*. Text copyright © 2017 by Derrik Barnes. Illustrations copyright © 2020 by Gordon C. James. Reproduced by permission of the publisher, Agate Publishing.

Lesson 2.5, image of planetary collision, credit: NASA/SOFIA/Lynette Cook *(pictured left);* credit: NASA/JPL-Caltech. Image of planetary collision *(pictured right)*.

Chapter 6

Cover and interior images from *Up, Up and Away, Monarch Butterflies* by Marta Magellan. Illustrated by Mauro Magellan. Photos by James Gersing. © 2024 by Marta Magellan. Reproduced with permission of the publisher, Eifrig Publishing.

Lesson 6.5, images from *Butterflies for Kids* by LearnBright. Reproduced with permission of the publisher. Original content found on LearnBright.org.

Index